THE SOVIET BALTIC OFFENSIVE, 1944–45

CASEMATE | ILLUSTRATED

☾ CASEMATE | ILLUSTRATED

THE SOVIET BALTIC OFFENSIVE, 1944–45

GERMAN DEFENSE OF ESTONIA, LATVIA, AND LITHUANIA

IAN BAXTER

CASEMATE | ILLUSTRATED

Acknowledgements: I wish to thank my artist Johnny Shumate for some of the illustrations in this book. I also want to thank my armored artist Oliver Missing for his time and expertise in producing some fine and well-detailed German and Soviet tanks, as well as the maps. Please find Oliver's vast selection of illustrations at his "Engines of WW2" site: www.o5m6.de.

CIS0024

Print Edition: ISBN 978-1-63624-106-7
Digital Edition: ISBN 978-1-63624-107-4

Design by Battlefield Design
Maps by Oliver Missing
Artwork by Johnny Shumate and Oliver Missing
Printed and bound in Turkey by Mega Print

CASEMATE PUBLISHERS (US)
Telephone (610) 853-9131
Fax (610) 853-9146
Email: casemate@casematepublishers.com
www.casematepublishers.com

CASEMATE PUBLISHERS (UK)
Telephone (01865) 241249
Email: casemate-uk@casematepublishers.co.uk
www.casematepublishers.co.uk

The photos in this book are derived from the author's personal collection or from archival sources, including the US National Archives and Records Administration, Library of Congress, Bundesarchiv, and the US Military History Institute.

Title page image: Red Army troops supported by advancing T-34 tanks during operations in the Baltics.
Contents page map: Map of the Baltic operation, January 1, 1944. (Ministry of Defence of USSR)
Contents page image: Exhausted Waffen-SS soldiers in a defensive position near the city of Narva, Estonia, February 1944. While the the battle for the city raged, Latvian SS tried to defend its lines against overwhelming superiority.

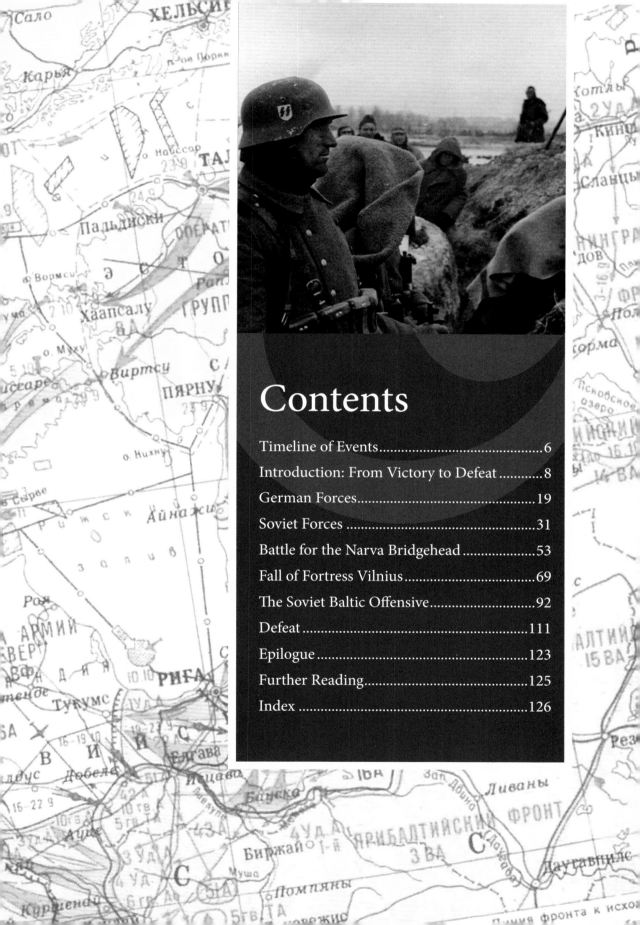

Contents

| Timeline of Events

December 30, 1943: Soviet planning for the "Estonian Operation," the winter campaign against German Army Group North, to secure Leningrad and break through the Narva Isthmus.

February 2, 1944: The battle of Narva opens. German "Army Detachment Narva" defense against Soviet Leningrad Front is solid.

February 11, 1944: Soviet 30th Guards Rifle Corps forces Narva bridgehead for several miles. German 227th and 170th Divisions retreat.

March 23, 1944: Army Detachment Narva clings on to the bridgehead as Soviet offensive bogs down with spring thaw.

June 23, 1944: Red Army unleashes Operation *Bagration*, the great summer offensive, against German Army Group Center. Army Group North forced to assist Third Panzer Army, thus diluting its strength.

July 1, 1944: Soviet 1st Baltic Front penetrates the weakened Army Group North to reach Latvian and Lithuanian frontiers.

July 13, 1944: In spite of fanatical resistance by the German garrison, "Fortress Vilnius" capitulates. The Germans suffer 13,000 casualties.

July 24, 1944: Soviet Leningrad Front launches a fresh offensive against Narva which is captured on the 26th. German forces fall back on Tannenberg Line in area of Sinimäed hills. Red Army efforts to destroy Tannenberg Line hampered by German counterattacks.

September 14, 1944: Soviet Baltic Offensive opens with the Riga Offensive, launched by the 1st, 2nd, and 3rd Baltic Fronts, to capture the Latvian capital Riga and cut off Army Group North in Courland in western Latvia and the Gulf of Riga.

September 17, 1944: Soviet 3rd Baltic Front launches Tallinn Offensive to encircle Army Detachment Narva but stiff resistance enables the Germans to consolidate on Latvian border.

Waffen-SS infantry take cover along a ditch at the side of a dusty road during a heavy Soviet attack during the summer of 1944.

A Soviet T-34-85 tank of the 119th Separate Tank Regiment belonging to the 1st Baltic Front during operations in March 1944. The 1st Baltic Front was committed to a number of important military operations on the Eastern Front, including assisting in lifting the siege of Leningrad on January 27, 1944.

September 22, 1944: Estonian capital Tallinn is abandoned. Soviet artillery pummels harbour at Haapsalu and Vormsi Island to prevent desperate German units from escaping by sea.

September 29, 1944: *Moonsund* landing operation, the amphibious attack by Soviet 8th Army, captures remaining islands off Estonian coast.

October 5, 1944: 1st Baltic Front launches the fourth element of the Baltic Offensive, forcing German formations west through Shaulyay into a narrow bridgehead at Memel. Riga attacked by heavy air and ground bombardments.

October 13, 1944: Riga falls to the 3rd Baltic Front. 33 divisions of Army Group North retreat to Courland peninsula, soon to be trapped in the Courland pocket.

December 21, 1944: Stiff German resistance during the "Christmas battles" in the Courland bridgehead halts Soviet 1st and 2nd Baltic Fronts with heavy casualties. German front stabilizes on New Year's Eve.

January 12/13, 1945: Red Army launches massive winter offensive to seal off East Prussia. Memel bridgehead destroyed.

January 28, 1945: German defense of Memel collapses. Remnants of three German divisions redeploy to defend Samland peninsula.

March 30, 1945: Red Army isolates Army Group North/Courland and drives through Lithuania into East Prussia. Danzig, Zoppot, and Gotenhafen are all captured.

May 8, 1945: Remnants of Army Group Courland officially surrender. Two days later, Leningrad Front captures Courland peninsula, and reaches Baltic coast.

Introduction: From Victory to Retreat

For the invasion of the Soviet Union, codenamed *Barbarossa*, the German Army assembled some three million men, in a total of 105 infantry divisions and 32 panzer divisions. This massive force was distributed between three German army groups.

Army Group North, commanded by General Wilhelm Ritter von Leeb, assembled in East Prussia on the Lithuanian frontier. Leeb's army group was to provide the main spearhead for the advance on Leningrad.

Army Group Center, commanded by General Fedor von Bock, assembled on the 1939 Polish/Russian frontier, both north and south of Warsaw. Bock's force consisted of 42 infantry divisions of the Fourth and Ninth Armies and II and III Panzer Groups. Of the three army groups this force contained the largest number of German infantry and panzer divisions.

Army Group South, commanded by General Gerd von Rundstedt, was deployed down the longest stretch of border with Russia. The front, reaching from central Poland to the Black Sea, was held by a panzer group, three German and two Rumanian armies, plus a Hungarian motorized corps, under German command.

A column of German vehicles, including a motorcyclist with sidecar combination, advances along a typical dirt road during the opening phase of the invasion of the Soviet Union in June 1941.

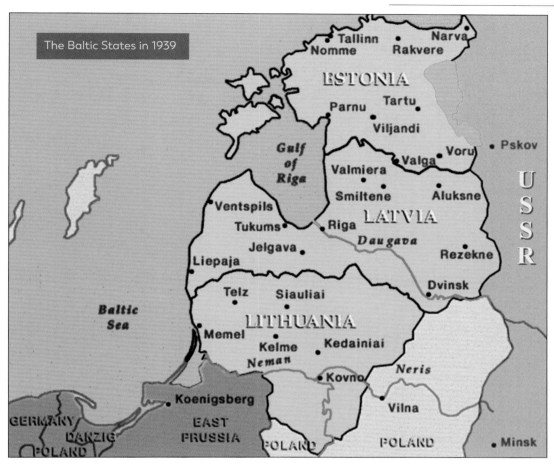

The Baltic States in 1939

Russian riflemen cling to the sides of advancing T-34 tank during an armored drive through Latvia in the early summer of 1944. Once the soldiers were nearing enemy lines they would dismount and charge into action.

Animal draught towing a 10.5cm howitzer to the front. General von Leeb's Army Group North was given the task of destroying the Red Army in the Baltic region.

Adolf Hitler had stipulated on the eve of the invasion that the objective in Army Group North was a thrust across East Prussia, smashing Soviet positions along the Baltic, liquidating the bases of the Baltic Fleet, destroying what was left of Russian naval power, and capturing Kronstadt and Leningrad. Once the latter had been razed to the ground, German armies could sweep down from the north while the main force closed in from the west. With half a million men at his disposal, comprising almost 30 divisions, six of them armored and motorized, Leeb was well placed to strike along the Baltic coast and dispose of the Soviet forces.

German troops sift through decimated Soviet lines looking for battlefield booty. Army Group North consisted of the Sixteenth and Eighteenth Armies, their objective Leningrad.

Halted in a Lithuanian town are a column of support vehicles on one side of the road and a line of halftracks hauling 15cm howitzers on the other. The 15cm gun was broken down into two loads. In this photograph the gun's tube and breech are transported on a special four-wheeled wagon.

Leeb's rapid two-pronged offensive opened at first light on the morning of June 22, 1941, his Sixteenth and Eighteenth Armies annihilating Soviet defenses along the border. Army Group North mechanically chewed its way through enemy positions, heading through Lithuania, Latvia, and Estonia, toward their objective: Leningrad. Within a few short weeks, Army Group North had broken through south of Pskov and was rolling toward Luga: they would need no more than nine or ten days to reach the outskirts of Leningrad. But following their initial surge of success, the Wehrmacht was losing momentum. Not only were supply lines being overstretched, but enemy resistance was beginning to stiffen on the

The same halftracks towing 15cm field howitzers. Whilst halftracks were more than capable of moving heavy weaponry quickly and effectively, much of the motive power in 1941 was still animal draught.

German infantry come across battlefield booty during their advance through Latvia. A soldier checks out a Soviet Maxim 1910 machine gun. The M1910 was mounted on a cumbersome wheeled mount with a gun shield; however, two years later, in 1943, it was replaced by the SG-43 Goryunov.

road to Leningrad. In a desperate attempt to blunt the German advance and prevent them from reaching the imperial city, brigades of Russian marines, naval units, and more than 80,000 men from the Baltic Fleet were hastily sent into action against Leeb's forces. These Soviet troops were now the sole barrier between Leningrad and the Germans. Although the German advance was hampered by this resistance, by the end of August 1941, Leeb's panzers were finally within sight of Leningrad. The terrified civilians left inside the city walls were about to endure one of the most brutal sieges in 20th-century history, a siege that was to last 872 days.

A column of Pz.Kpfw. IIIs stopped along a road during a pause in Army Group North's advance. The army group that invaded the Baltics consisted of some half a million men in almost 30 divisions, six of them armored and motorized with 1,500 Panzers and 12,000 heavy weapons, plus an air fleet of nearly 1,000 planes.

As the summer of 1941 passed and the Germans drew closer to the city gates, Leningraders were issued grim orders to defend their city to the death. Although Leeb's forces had arrived within shelling distance of Leningrad, the advance had not gone entirely as planned, mired as they were on the Leningrad Front by stiffening resistance. Leeb was now under considerable pressure from Hitler to complete his assignment of encircling Leningrad, to join forces with the Finns, and destroy the Baltic Fleet. His forces were desperately needed for the Moscow front, where the Wehrmacht was preparing to go in for the kill and capture the capital. But despite assurances from Leeb that he was making good progress, German troops were still facing hundreds of miles of earth walls, antitank ditches, and wire barricades, thousands of defensive pill-boxes, and the harrying activities of Soviet tanks outside the city.

By September 1941 the situation for Army Group North was increasingly troubling as there were now no strategic reserves to rely upon. So, instead, the Germans decided to surround Leningrad and starve the city into submission, rather than undertake costly assaults against a growing and determined enemy. Army Group North had allowed itself to be drawn across vast, unending terrain, overstretching resources and supply lines. And the onset of a bitter winter was wreaking havoc with the ill-prepared invaders.

Over the following months, fighting in Army Group North continued, but much of its forces had stagnated. Leningrad continued to hold out in what became known as the siege of Leningrad, and German units found themselves either sitting in trenches for weeks on end or continuously embroiled in heavy defensive or offensive fighting. Most of Army Group North was situated along what was known as the Panther-Wotan Line, a defensive

A column of StuG. IIIs halted on a road in Latvia. For the invasion of Russia, German factories produced 548 StuG. III vehicles which were distributed across the three army groups. The StuG had a crew of four and came equipped with a 7.5cm StuK 37 L/24 gun capable of traversing from 12.5° left to 12.5° right. With the vehicle's low silhouette for better survivability, it not only provided sterling offensive service, but performed well during defensive battles as well.

In Profile:
German and Soviet Tank Men

Pz.Kpfw.35(t), 6th Panzer Division, June 1941. This panzer is finished in overall dark gray and carries the divisional insignia of two yellow-painted XXs. (Oliver Missing)

KV-1 Model, Leningrad Front, October 1941. This Soviet tank is camouflaged in overall dark green. This heavy tank was equipped with a long-barrel 76.2mm ZIS-5 gun that could penetrate the armor of the German tank of the same period from a long distance. (Oliver Missing)

line partially built by the Wehrmacht. This defensive barrier ran between Lake Peipus and the Baltic Sea at Narva. The rest of the line stretched south toward the Black Sea, along the Dnieper River. Many of these German lines consisted of mazes of intricate blockhouses and trenches. Towns that fell in the path of these defensive belts were evacuated. Thousands of women, children, and old men were removed from their dwellings with many pressed into service to help construct massive antitank trenches and other obstacles.

A typical strongpoint along the front contained light and heavy MG 34 and MG 42 machine guns, an antitank rifle company or battalion, a sapper platoon equipped with a host of various explosives, infantry guns, an antitank artillery company with a number of antitank guns, and occasionally a self-propelled gun.

Operating at intervals were Pz.Kpfw. IV, Tiger, and Panther tanks, and a number of StuG. III assault guns, all of which had been scraped together. This front-line belt was designated as a killing zone where every possible antitank weapon and artillery piece would be used to ambush Soviet tanks. Whilst an enemy tank was subjected to a storm of fire within the kill zone, special mobile engineer detachments equipped with anti-personnel and antitank mines would quickly deploy and erect new obstacles, just in case any enemy tanks managed to escape the zone. If the crew of a disabled tank survived the initial attack and bailed out, special sapper units were ordered to pick off any survivors. Behind these defensive positions at varying depths were antitank defenses, including mortars, Panzerschreck, Panzerfaust, and 7.5cm and 8.8cm Flak guns, ready to counter any enemy armored vehicle that managed to break through.

But in spite of these heavily fortified areas, the Soviet Army was steadily growing in size and causing additional strain on the German lines. By the end of 1943, as the military situation on the Eastern Front further deteriorated, Army Group staff planned to abandon

A 15cm field howitzer crew during a lull in the fighting near Leningrad. By mid-September, the Moscow front could wait no longer for an Army Group North victory. The powerful XXXXI Panzer Corps was redeployed to the Moscow front, upsetting the dynamics of Leeb's force.

Armor and support vehicles cross a heavy pontoon bridge known by the Germans as a *Bruckengerat B*. The pontoon boats have been lashed together with the bridging deck sections secured over them.

these lines for a new position to the rear that would shorten the front lines by 25 percent and remove the Soviet threats posed along their existing front. The plan called for a January withdrawal of over 150 miles to the natural defensive barrier formed by the Narva and Velikaya Rivers and Lakes Peipus and Pskov. Hitler, however, rejected all proposals for an early withdrawal into the Panther position, insisting that the Red Army was to be contained if it unleashed an offensive.

On January 27, 1944, the Red Army did indeed launch an offensive. The attack, known as the Leningrad–Novgorod Offensive, was undertaken by the Soviet Volkhov and Leningrad Fronts with elements of the 2nd Baltic Front. The attack was so heavy that it saw the Germans suffer nearly 72,000 casualties, including the loss of 85 artillery pieces. In the following days the Soviets pushed Army Group North from the Volkhov River to the Gulf of Finland which was littered with a string of trenches and shell holes, reminiscent of the trench warfare in World War I. The German Eighteenth Army bore the brunt of the attack and was vastly outnumbered in both infantry and armor. As usual German troops were expected to hold the front, but overwhelming enemy firepower proved too much and the Eighteenth Army was compelled to fall back some 50 miles from Leningrad to the Luga River under a hurricane of enemy fire.

As the offensive gathered momentum a chain reaction of events saw German divisions in their dozens withdraw from their lines of trenches and fortifications back across a scarred and devastated wasteland toward the borders of the Baltic states of Estonia, Latvia, and Lithuania. It was here the German troops were ordered to "stand and fight" and wage an unprecedented battle of attrition in what became known as the battle of the Baltics.

Troops during the first winter of 1941/2 prepare to move out of a village with horse-drawn transport. By this stage of the war, although Army Group North had managed to advance to the outskirts of Leningrad, all available resources had been drawn down and the front had stagnated.

German Forces

By 1944 the German soldier in Army Group North had become accustomed to the determined, fanatical resistance of the Red Army. At the same time, they had destroyed the warmth and goodwill of the people of Estonia, Latvia, and Estonia – most of whom would be only too glad to be rid of Nazi rule. For the general populace the Soviets were the lesser of two evils.

The German soldier was all too well aware of the dire military situation in the Baltic region. The days of high optimism, with young, enthusiastic, fresh-faced marching soldiers convinced of their ability as they stepped out east, were long gone. Now, as they withdrew westward from Russia into the Baltic states, many Germans, both officers and men, were faced with situations for which no solutions had been given other than stand fast and fight to the death. For months many of these soldiers had lived and fought along lines of fortifications and barricades and often led a life of inactivity other than occasionally going into action against the growing might of the Red Army, or undertaking probing attacks around Leningrad. However, the Red Army had now gathered momentum and was recapturing more and more towns and villages. Many isolated German units spent hours or even days fighting a bloody defense. Russian soldiers frequently requested them to surrender and assured them that no harm would come to them if they did, but most German troops continued to fight to the bitter end. To the German soldier in 1944 they were fighting an enemy that they not only despised, but were also terrified of. Many soldiers, especially those in the ranks of the Waffen-SS, decided that their fate would be met out on the battlefield; they would

A German 15cm howitzer along the stagnated front. A sense of futility and gloom gripped the German soldiers, thousands of whom had been killed. By mid-October 1942, they found themselves substantially in the same position they had been in during spring.

rather bleed to death fighting than surrender and be at the mercy of a Russian soldier. All were ordered to stand and fight and not abandon their positions. Yet, the overwhelming superiority of the Red Army saw thousands of German soldiers retreat to the borders of the Baltic states where new defenses were erected.

Elements of a Typical German Division, 1944

Infantry Division

By 1944 the infantry division had gone through a series of changes and had been modified and reorganized. The reconnaissance battalion, for instance, was removed and replaced by a bicycle-mounted reconnaissance platoon in every regiment. The antitank battalion was more or less motorized and consisted of an antitank company equipped with Jagdpanzer IVs, Hetzers, or StuGs, which were organized into three platoons of four vehicles and an HQ section of two vehicles, a motorized antitank company of 12 x 7.5cm PaK 40 guns and a motorized flak company equipped with 12 x 2cm or 3.7cm flak guns. The engineer battalion also took over the responsibility of the heavy weapons company, which was comprised of three engineer companies, each equipped with two 81cm mortars, two machine guns and six portable flamethrowers. The heavy weapons in the engineer battalion were normally mounted in trucks, but by 1944 they were predominately pulled by animal draught, whilst the troops were mounted on bicycles.

At regimental level an antitank company was added. This consisted of a platoon equipped with three 5cm PaK 38 guns and two platoons armed with Panzerfausts. Within the regiments, the infantry battalions were reduced to just two. A number of divisions in the field received fusilier battalions which were identically structured to the new standard rifle battalion. The infantry battalions were equipped with four 12cm heavy mortars, whilst the rifle company's heavy weapons platoon was equipped with two 8.1cm mortars.

StuG. IIIs advance along to the front, late 1943. By this time Army Group North's tactical position had become very fragile as the Soviets were preparing their massive offensive aimed at crushing the Germans and driving them out of the Soviet Union and the Baltic states.

Panzergrenadier Division

By 1944 many infantry divisions were redesignated as panzergrenadier divisions. Although having an armored designation, the panzergrenadier division was still technically an infantry formation. However, unlike a normal infantry division there was a higher-than-usual attachment of armored vehicles. A typical panzergrenadier division had at least one battalion of infantry that was transported to the forward edge of the battlefield by Sd.kfz.251 halftracks, with armored support provided by its own StuG battalion. A typical panzergrenadier division was normally composed of an HQ company, a motorized engineer battalion and two panzergrenadier regiments. Invariably, the division had a StuG battalion, which contained an HQ platoon equipped with three StuGs and three StuG companies. The StuG battalion was normally supported by a company comprising a StuG platoon which was equipped with four StuGs with 10.5cm guns, a flak platoon with three quad 2cm guns mounted on Sd.Kfz.6 or 7 halftracks, an armored engineer platoon with five Sd.Kfz.250 halftracks, and a motorized signal platoon. Other support elements with the division comprised the following:

Artillery Regiment

3 x 2cm flak guns (towed by howitzer battalion)

3 x 2cm flak guns

4 x 15cm sFH 18 howitzers

4 x 10.5cm leFH 18 howitzers

1 battery of 6 x Hummels

2 batteries of 6 x Wespes

1 company of 14 x Jagdpanzers

15 x 7.5cm PaK 40 vehicle-towed guns

1 company of 12 x quad flak 2cm guns

2 companies of 4 x 8.8cm guns

Armored Reconnaissance Battalion

4 platoons of 4 x Sd.Kfz.231s

MG platoons of 4 x MG 34/42s (on sustained fire mounts)

3 x rifle platoons

Armored Reconnaissance Battalion Support

2 x 7.5cm leIG 18 guns

3 x 5cm PaK 38 guns

1 x engineer platoon

Panzer/Panzergrenadier Brigade

By the summer of 1944, as the situation in the East deteriorated, Hitler outlined that his commanders needed small, mobile, fast armored *Kampfgruppen*—battle groups—which could be used effectively to meet attacking enemy armored formations. During the first week of July plans were issued to create these special armored *Kampfgruppen*, to consist of at least one SPW (*Schützenpanzerwagen*) battalion, one panzer group with some 40 panzers, one Pak company and a number of flak wagons. In total about 12 such *Kampfgruppen*, named panzer brigades, were to be attached to combat units on the Eastern Front.

On 11 July, OKH issued orders to create 10 panzer brigades, designated Panzer-Brigade 101 to 110. Each brigade had one panzer *Abteilung* with three Panther companies and one panzerjager company, and one panzergrenadier battalion with four companies.

Panzer Division

15,943 men

91 x Pz.Kpfw. IV (7.5cm L/48 guns) medium tanks

90 x Panther (7.5cm L/70 guns) medium tanks

42 x Hetzer (7.5cm L/48 guns) tank destroyers

9 x 15cm FH 18/40 towed howitzers

18 x 10.5cm leF 18 towed howitzers

6 x 15cm self-propelled sIG infantry guns

12 x 7.5cm PaK 40 towed antitank guns

36 x 5cm PaK 39 towed antitank guns

A StuG. III advances through one of the many villages along the front.

14 x 8.8cm Flak 36 towed antiaircraft guns

12 x 3.7cm Flak 36 towed antiaircraft guns

13 x 2cm towed antiaircraft guns

32 x 7.5cm leIG 37 and sIG 33 towed infantry guns

80 x 8.1cm mortars

570 x machine guns

48 x Sd.Kfz.232 and 263 armored cars

1,000 x trucks

Divisional Reconnaissance Battalion

(A battalion varied from unit to unit)

1 x signals platoon

1 x halftrack company

1 x light halftrack company

1 x halftrack reconnaissance company

1 x heavy company of 6 x 80cm mortars and 6 x 7.5cm guns.

In 1944 the formation of the antitank battalion was changed to 12 x 7.5cm PaK and 14 x self-propelled antitank guns in two companies, each of three platoons. Antiaircraft cover for the division was provided by an antiaircraft battalion, comprised of an antiaircraft company with 12 x 2cm flak guns in three platoons and most importantly 8.8cm guns in two companies of four to six guns each. By the latter period of the war the famous 8.8cm guns were increasingly employed in the antitank role to combat the threat of heavier Soviet tanks.

Tiger Battalion

The Tiger and King Tiger were never officially integrated into the divisional organization. They were maintained in separate battalions. There was no tank platoon at battalion HQ. Each company was comprised of 14 tanks divided between a HQ with two vehicles and three platoons each with four vehicles.

Assault Gun Battalion

The assault gun (*Sturmgeschütz*) was used originally to provide infantry support. However, as the situation in the East deteriorated, they were issued to panzergrenadier divisions to support and equip their single panzer battalion. They were also utilized in antitank battalions as well. But as losses increasingly mounted, they were moved into the panzer battalions, regularly equipping and supporting panzer companies into battle.

Kampfgruppe

A *Kampfgruppe* varied in strength from a corps to a company size. The *Kampfgruppe* was essentially an ad hoc organization of various arms and utilized different arms for specific

In Profile:
Pz.Kpfw. IV Ausf.G and SS Panzergrenadier

A Pz.Kpfw. IV operating in Latvia in the summer of 1944. This vehicle is finished in dark sand base. It has a textbook camouflage scheme of green and brown patches applied over the whole vehicle, including the back-fitted turret and hull *schurzen* (side skirts). Mesh has been attached over its *schurzen* to combat magnetic mines being attached to the hull, and for additional camouflage purposes. Foliage has also been applied to the tank in order to break up its distinctive shape. (Oliver Missing)

Waffen-SS Estonian volunteer, summer 1944. He wears the Waffen-SS tunic complete with a cloth face mask made of the same material as his tunic. He is armed with a captured PPSh-41 "Shpagin's" machine pistol. (Johnny Shumate)

operational tasks. These tasks could either be short or long term and were often organized quickly in relation to the tactical or strategic situation. *Kampfgruppen* were typically named after the person chosen to command the formation. The concept of the *Kampfgruppe* was a key element in German tactical doctrine by 1944.

German Heavy Tank Company

The heavy tank company, or *Schwere Panzerkompanie*, was intended to be fitted out with Tiger I or Tiger II tanks, as opposed to medium tank companies which were intended to utilize Panthers, Pz.Kpfw. IVs or Pz.Kpfw. IV/70 tank destroyers. By 1944 the heavy tank company was regarded as the main armored striking element of a heavy tank battalion or *Schwere Panzer-Abteilung*. Each heavy tank battalion element comprised one staff company, one workshop company and three heavy tank companies.

Company Headquarters

Tank 1 (Tiger I or Tiger II)

1 x company leader (*Kompanieführer*), *Hauptmann*

1 x gunner (*Richtschützen*), *Unteroffizier* to *Feldwebel*

1 x driver (Kraftwagenfahrer), *Unteroffizier* to *Feldwebel*

1 x radio operator (*Funker*), *Unteroffizier* to *Feldwebel*

1 x loader (*Ladeschützen*), *Panzerschütze* to *Obergefreiter*

Tank 2 (Tiger I or Tiger II)

1x tank commander (*Kommandant*), *Unteroffizier* to *Feldwebel*

1x gunner, *Unteroffizier* to *Feldwebel*

1x driver, *Unteroffizier* to *Feldwebel*

1x radio operator, *Panzerschütze* to *Obergefreiter*

1x loader, *Panzerschütze* to *Obergefreiter*

Administrative Personnel

1 x administrative first sergeant (*Hauptfeldwebel*), *Oberfeldwebel*

1 x weapons NCO (*Waffenunteroffizier*), *Unteroffizier* to *Feldwebel*

2 x messengers—Kettenkrad (*Kradmelder*), *Panzerschütze* to *Obergefreiter*

1 x messenger (*Melder*), *Panzerschütze* to *Obergefreiter*

2 x drivers for cars (*Kraftwagenfahrer für Pkw*), *Panzerschütze* to *Obergefreiter*

Additional Equipment

2 x Kettenkrad halftrack motorcycles

2 x Kübelwagen cars

Three Platoons

Tank 1 (Tiger I or Tiger II)

1 x platoon leader (*Zugführer*), *Leutnant*

1 x gunner, *Unteroffizier* to *Feldwebel*

1 x driver, *Unteroffizier* to *Feldwebel*

1 x radio operator, *Unteroffizier* to *Feldwebel*

1 x loader, *Panzerschütze* to *Obergefreiter*

Tank 2 (Tiger I or Tiger II)

1 x deputy platoon leader (*Stellvertreter Zugführer*), *Unteroffizier* to *Feldwebel*

1 x gunner, *Unteroffizier* to *Feldwebel*

1 x driver, *Unteroffizier* to *Feldwebel*

1 x radio operator, *Panzerschütze* to *Obergefreiter*

1 x loader, *Panzerschütze* to *Obergefreiter*

Tank 3 (Tiger I or Tiger II)

1 x vehicle commander, *Unteroffizier* to *Feldwebel*

1 x gunner, *Unteroffizier* to *Feldwebel*

1 x driver, *Unteroffizier*

Winter-clad Army Group North troops trudge through the snow as their forces are pushed back by the Russian winter offensive of January 1944, directed against them by the Leningrad and Volkhov Fronts.

1 x radio operator, *Panzerschütze* to *Obergefreiter*

1 x loader, *Panzerschütze* to *Obergefreiter*

Tank 4 (Tiger I or Tiger II)

1 x vehicle commander, *Unteroffizier* to *Feldwebel*

1 x gunner, *Panzerschütze* to *Obergefreiter*

1 x driver, *Unteroffizier* to *Feldwebel*

1 x radio operator, *Panzerschütze* to *Obergefreiter*

1 x loader, *Panzerschütze* to *Obergefreiter*

Spare Crews

2 x vehicle commanders, *Unteroffizier* to *Feldwebel*

2 x drivers, *Unteroffizier* to *Feldwebel*

2 x gunners, *Panzerschütze* to *Obergefreiter*

2 x radio operators, *Panzerschütze* to *Obergefreiter*

2 x loaders, *Panzerschütze* to *Obergefreiter*

A German Wespe self-propelled gun advances across the snow during the Red Army winter offensive. The German Eighteenth Army was outnumbered by at least 3:1 in divisions, 3:1 in artillery, and 6:1 in tanks, self-propelled artillery, and aircraft.

German Commanders

General Walter Model

Model was urgently sent to command Army Group North at the end of January 1944. He was a great improviser and used his military expertise with brutal effect. As a result of his ingenuity and tough discipline, he temporarily restored the front as the German forces stepped back to defend the Panther-Wotan Line. As his troops withdrew, he delegated responsibility for the Narva front to General Johannes Friessner commanding Army Detachment Narva, while he concentrated on extricating Eighteenth Army with as few casualties as possible. By the end of March Model was removed from Army Group North to southern Russia, but his skill and tenacity on the battlefield had saved many lives.

General Georg Lindemann

Lindemann was promoted to command Army Group North on March 31, 1944. As a commander he was aware of his capabilities; however, the task he had to try and contain the Red Army was too much for him and on July 4 was relieved of his command and transferred to the Reserve Army.

General Johannes Friessner

In February 1944, Friessner was transferred to the Northern Front and assigned command of the Sponheimer Group, which was later renamed Army Detachment Narva, on February 23, 1944. In early July he was briefly given the command of Army Group North before being sent to the Southern Front to command Army Group South Ukraine.

General Field Marshal Walter Model.

General Georg Lindemann. (Bundesarchiv Bild 183-L08017)

General Johannes Friessner. (Bundesarchiv Bild 146-1984-018-27A)

General Herbert Loch
(on the right).
(Bundesarchiv Bild 183-
B10901)

General Ferdinand Schörner

Schörner was commonly known as a simple disciplinarian and a dedicated Nazi who was wholly obedient to Hitler's defensive orders. On the battlefield he was a talented leader with exceptional organizational ability who managed his troops well, especially in a defensive role. In July 1944, he became commander of Army Group North where he displayed energy and charisma. However, he was also brutal in upholding his Führer's orders, and those who did not follow orders were either removed from the front or court-martialled on the spot; deserters were hanged if found guilty. In January 1944, Schörner was transferred to command Army Group Center.

General Herbert Loch

Photographed during a parade ceremony are Loch (right) and General Maximilian von Weichs. Loch was a very capable and committed general, popular with his troops. He was given the command of the Eighteenth Army following Lindemann's promotion to commander Army Group North. He held the command until September 2, 1944, blamed by Hitler for the military reverses of the Eighteenth Army.

General Ehrenfried Boege

On September 5, 1944, Boege was given the command of the Eighteenth Army, a post that many commanders would have been reluctant to take. However, his vigor and experience enabled him to excel, especially during operations in the Courland pocket where some 200,000 troops belonging to the Sixteenth and Eighteenth Armies had become trapped.

Left: General Ferdinand Schörner. (Bundesarchiv Bild 183-L29176)

Right: General Ehrenfried Boege.

29

General Christian Hansen. (Bundesarchiv Bild 146-1971-035-88)

General Paul Laux.

General Carl Hilpert.

General Christian Hansen

Hansen was commander of Sixteenth Army in 1944 and was recipient of the Knights Cross of the Iron Cross, awarded for extreme battlefield bravery and for his successful military leadership. But by the summer of 1944, as his forces tried to hold their positions against the overwhelming might of the Red Army, his unit sustained high losses. As a result, he was blamed for the military setback, but could do nothing to avert the situation as his forces had been ordered to stand and fight.

General Paul Laux

Hitler blamed General Hansen for the Sixteenth Army's predicament and replaced him with General Laux on July 11, 1944. He was regarded as one of the most brilliant Eastern Front tacticians of the war. However, his command was short-lived: on August 29, 1944, during a reconnaissance flight, his aircraft crashed. He died of his injuries four days later, on September 2.

General Carl Hilpert

Hilpert was a well-decorated tactician and his success on the battlefield saw him take command of the Sixteenth Army in September 1944. From September until the end of March 1945, Hilpert planned the breakout of his army trapped in the Courland pocket, but all attempts were in vain.

Soviet Forces

By 1944 Soviet troops were masters of both defense and offense. They had overcome their mistakes very quickly and learned German tactics which they were able to adapt on the battlefield. They were now competent to attack enemy lines in depth with tanks and supporting infantry, often overtaking retreating German units and cutting them off. The principle of attacking in depth was the Soviet response to the increased capability and mobility of fire support systems such as artillery and aviation, and the massed mechanized infantry, tank, and airborne forces.

Soviet fire support could now reach farther, and the Red Army tank and infantry formations had increased in mobility. Simultaneous artillery attacks and airstrikes through the entire depth of enemy defenses, combined with thousands of tank and infantry formations, often simply overwhelmed the Germans.

The Russian soldier was fully prepared to accomplish the mission regardless of loss of life and under any military conditions. Soldiers were indoctrinated to achieve surprise whenever possible. All military operations were characterized by decisiveness and aggressiveness. Each soldier now strove continuously to seize and hold the initiative,

Russian POWs being led away to a fate that can only be imagined. The bulk of the Russian POWs that survived the prison camps in the East were transported to Poland and Germany where they were put to work in concentration camps. By 1943, many were working in the armaments industry in appalling conditions. The majority did not survive.

and make full use of all available military assets and capabilities to achieve victory for the Motherland. During an attack, soldiers were to ensure that major formations and units of all services, branches, and arms effected thorough and continuous coordination and selected the principal enemy objective to be seized and the best routes for attacking it. As a result of these mass attacks, German lines of communication, and command and control were destroyed or disrupted as the remainder of the forward edge of their lines fragmented and collapsed. Disorganized, demoralized, and isolated, German commanders were often unable to re-establish an effective and coordinated defense and were forced to withdraw or become cut off. These successful, high-speed, deep, aggressive operations were now part of the Soviet soldier's doctrine for victory.

The Red Army was more than prepared to exert itself at great expense to achieve its goals. Its tolerance for sacrifice was high, which they believed would be the only way to bring about victory against their invaders.

Another element of success for the Red Army in 1944 was mass combined reserves which were made up of tank, motorized rifle, and artillery subunits. When a large single echelon was employed in an attack, a combined arms reserve would then be moved up and used to exploit any success. Its advance was often similar to the initial front-line attack, but normally without a preassigned mission. The reserves were used primarily for security and reaction to enemy counterattack. Special reserves were organized from antitank, engineer, or other combat support elements, and were used primarily for defense against enemy counterattacks, security, and tasks requiring more specialized skills.

Furthermore, the Germans often forgot to appreciate the Soviet ability to recognize and understand their enemy's (the Germans') fragile military situation. They were aware that the Germans considered their northern sector less threatened than other sectors of the front. The German soldier had built hundreds of miles of trenches, fortifications, and barricades, and as such there were significant areas that had witnessed barely any fighting. The Russians were determined to take advantage of these areas and launch deep, penetrative

Troops of Army Group North operating in the snow, early winter 1942. The harsh winter conditions enabled Russian forces to build up their lines of defense and prepare for the spring thaw.

attacks, and were able to inflict heavy losses on their enemy who had little in the way of reserves and was unable to flood the front with fresh reinforcements. As a result, when the Soviets launched their attacks, they came as a surprise; as a consequence the Germans were compelled to withdraw from the front lines in order to save their units from complete annihilation, Wehrmacht units retreated along the borders of the Baltic states, which became the springboard for the Red Army to march into East Prussia and the Reich.

Elements of a Typical Soviet Division, 1944

Infantry Company

Command Group

Company commander

2 x snipers

Messenger

Clerk

Sergeant-major

Observer

Medical NCO

2 x Infantry Platoons

Platoon leader

3 x infantry groups

Group leader

Assistant group leader

Automatic rifleman with automatic rifle

3 x riflemen

50mm Mortar Platoon

Platoon leader

2 x mortar groups

Mortar leader

Gunner with 50mm mortar

Mortar man

Machine-gun Group

Group leader

Assistant group leader/machine-gunner with machine gun

Assistant machine-gunner

2 x machine-gun men

Cart handler with horse and cart

Total Weaponry

27 x automatic rifles

2 x sniper rifles

23 x SMGs

6 x automatic rifles

1 x machine gun

2 x 50mm mortars

Motorized Infantry Regiment

Regimental commander

Deputy commander

Political deputy

Political deputy secretary

Political Department

Party secretary

Komsomol secretaries (3)

Propaganda director

Staff (16 men)

Chief of Staff

1st chief of staff assistants (4 men)

2nd chief of staff assistant (cryptography)

3rd chief of staff assistant (signals commander)

Signals commander's assistant

Staff officer

2nd-class translator

Senior clerk

Drawer

Artillery officer

Regimental engineer

Chemical defense officer

Senior doctor

Supply Departments (11 men)

Regiment commander's assistant (Supply)

Regiment commander's assistant (Technical Supply)

Combat supply

Technical supply

Column and personal equipment supply

Food supply

Cashier

Command Platoon (22 men)

Staff commandant

Sergeant-major

Command group

Group leader

2 x machine-gunners

4 x riflemen

Truck driver

Supply group (12 men)

3 x cooks

Private

7 x truck drivers

Motorcycle man

Reconnaissance Company (44 men)

Company commander

Political officer

2 x armored car drivers

2 x radiomen

Motorcycle Reconnaissance Platoon (10 men)

Platoon leader

Scout

Motorcycle Reconnaissance Group

Group leader

7 x motorcycle scouts

BA-20 Armored Car Platoon (12 men)

Platoon leader

3 x armored car commanders

4 x armored car drivers

3 x machine-gunners

1 x machine-gunner

BA-10 Armored Car Platoon (16 men)

Platoon leader

3 x armored car commanders

4 x gunners

4 x armored car drivers

4 x machine-gunners

Signals Company (68 men)

Company commander

Assistant company commander

Political officer

Sergeant-major

Truck driver

Staff Platoon (20 men)

Platoon leader

Telephone and signal flash station

Air defense observation post

Motorcycle messenger group

Radio Platoon (20 men)

Platoon leader

1 11-AK radio station (10 men)

1 5-AK radio station

2 6-PK radio station

Telephone and Signal Flash Platoon (14 men)

Platoon leader

2 x telephone and signal flash groups

Antiaircraft Machine-gun Company (38 men)

Company commander

Deputy company commander

Political officer

Sergeant-major

2 x radiomen

Motorcycle messenger

2 x Antiaircraft Machine-gun Platoons (16 men each)

Platoon leader

3 x group leaders

9 x machine-gun men

3 x car drivers

3 x AA machine guns

3 x trucks

Engineer Platoon (32 men)

Platoon leader

Engineer group

Group leader

7 x engineers

2 x engineer groups

Group leader

6 x engineers

Water collection group

Transport group

Traffic Guidance Platoon (19 men)

Platoon leader

2 x traffic guidance groups

Group leaders

4 x traffic guiders

2 x truck drivers

2 x motorcycle messengers

3 x Motorized Infantry Battalions (739 men each)

Battalion commander

Political officer

Staff (4 men)

Senior adjutant

Adjutant's assistant

Chemical defense director

Observer

Signals Platoon (21 men)

Platoon leader

Truck driver

Telephone and signal flash station

Radio group

Motorcycle Reconnaissance Platoon (17 men)

Platoon leader

2 x reconnaissance groups

Group leader

7 x motorcycle reconnaissance men

3 x Infantry Companies (190 men each)

Company commander

Political officer

Transport group

Group leader

11 x truck drivers

Command group

Sergeant-major

Equipment master

Medical NCO

3 x medics

Gunsmith

Sniper

3 x Infantry Platoons (47 men each)

Platoon Leader

Assistant platoon leader

Messenger

4 x infantry groups

Group leader

Assistant group leader

2 x automatic riflemen

7 x riflemen

Machine-gun Platoon (17 men)

Platoon leader

Assistant platoon leader

2 x machine-gun groups

Group leader

7 x machine-gun men

Mortar group

Group leader

9 x mortar men

3 x 50mm mortar

Machine-gun Company (72 men)

Company commander

Political officer

Command group

Sergeant-major

Observer

Group leader

3 x telephone men

3 x Machine-gun Platoons (19 men each)

Platoon leader

2 x machine-gun groups

Group leader

8 x machine-gun men

Transport group

Group leader

6 x truck drivers

Mortar Platoon (11 men)

Platoon leader

2 x mortar groups

Group leader

1 x direction finder

2 x mortar men

Truck driver

2 x 82mm mortars

Antitank Artillery Platoon (17 men)

Platoon leader

Observer

Truck driver

2 x antitank artillery groups

Gun leader

5 x gunners

Cart handlers

Truck driver

Supply Platoon (26 men)

Platoon leader

Combat supply group

Supply group

Truck workshop

Total Battalion Strength: 739 men each

2 x 45mm antitank guns

2 x 82mm mortars

9 x 50mm mortars

12 x machine-guns

38 x automatic rifles

324 x rifles

72 x automatic loading rifles

48 x sniper rifles

75 x pistols

35 x trucks

5 x field kitchens

1 x special vehicle (workshop truck)

Artillery Company (65 men)

4 x 76mm regimental cannons

Musicians (13 men)

Supply (129 men) (all units)

Total Regimental Strength: 2,677 men

4 x 76mm regimental cannons

6 x 45mm antitank guns

6 x 82mm mortars

27 x 50mm mortars

36 x machine guns

6 x AA machine guns (7.62mm)

122 x automatic rifles

111 x rifles with rifle grenade attachments

1,445 x rifles

216 x automatic loading rifles

144 x sniper rifles

520 x pistols

2 x cars

22 x special vehicles

236 x trucks

51 x motorcycles with sidecars with automatic rifles

19 x motorcycles

19 x field kitchens

10 x armored cars

Rifle Company

The rifle company was the close combat element of the rifle battalion, and was the main attacking force of the rifle regiment of the rifle division/Guards rifle division. Generally, the rifle company was comprised of one company HQ, two rifle platoons, one submachine-gun platoon, one medical section, one mortar platoon and one machine-gun section.

Company Headquarters

1 x company commander, captain.

1x company sergeant-major

1x quartermaster clerk, sr. sergeant

Medical Section

1 x medical instructor, senior sergeant

4 x medics, private

2 x Rifle Platoons

1 x platoon commander, jr. lieutenant or lieutenant

1 x deputy platoon commander, sr. sergeant

2 x snipers

2 x Light Rifle Sections

1 x section commander, jr. sergeant or sergeant

1 x deputy section commander (senior rifleman)

1 x light machine-gunner, private

1 x assistant machine-gunner, private

1 x rifleman

4 x riflemen

2 x Heavy Rifle Sections

1 x section commander, jr. sergeant or sergeant

1 x deputy section commander (senior rifleman)

2 x light machine-gunners

2 x assistant machine-gunners

1 x rifleman

2 x riflemen, private

1 x Submachine-gun Platoon

1 x platoon commander, jr. lieutenant or lieutenant

1 x deputy platoon commander, sr. sergeant

2 x snipers, private

2 x Light Rifle Sections

1 x section commander, jr. sergeant or sergeant

1 x deputy section commander (senior rifleman)

1 x light machine-gunner

1 x assistant machine-gunner

5 x riflemen

2 x Heavy Rifle Sections

1 x section commander, jr. sergeant or sergeant

1 x deputy section commander (senior rifleman)

2 x light machine-gunners, private

2 x assistant machine-gunners

3 x riflemen

1 x Machine-gun Section

1 x section commander, jr. sergeant

1 x machine-gunner

3 x ammunition bearers

1 x horse driver

Additional Equipment

1x draft horse and cart

1 x Mortar Platoon

1 x platoon commander, sr. sergeant

2 x Mortar Sections

1 x mortar man

2 x ammunition bearers

A knocked-out Russian T-34 tank near Leningrad, September 1941. Although the German advance was hampered by robust Soviet armored forces, by the end of August, Leeb's panzers were within sight of Leningrad.

Rifle Platoons

The rifle platoon generally comprised a platoon headquarters and four rifle sections. The platoon was led by a lieutenant platoon commander who was assisted by the deputy platoon commander. By early 1944, the primary weapon of a platoon commander was a submachine gun. There were two platoon-level snipers, equipped with the M1891/30 Mosin-Nagant with the PU scope. These snipers were intended to operate in pairs. The rifle sections comprised two heavy rifle sections and two light rifle sections and were regularly seen armed with the SVT-40 semi-automatic rifle. Riflemen were also armed with a submachine gun and would have been given the task of assaulting enemy positions. A heavy rifle section was also armed with two DP-27 light machine guns and a light rifle section was armed with one DP-27.

Submachine-gun Platoons

The submachine-gun platoon was a new addition by 1944. It was comprised of two heavy sections and one light section of the PPSh-41, but with all rifle-armed personnel.

A knocked-out T-34 tank along the Leningrad Front in the winter of 1941/2.

In Profile:
Soviet ISU-152S Heavy Self-Propelled Gun and Submachine-gunner

This ISU-152S heavy self-propelled gun has received a coating of whitewash camouflage paint over the entire vehicle. Although the vehicle was used as mobile artillery to support mobile infantry and armor attacks, it was also an effective heavy tank destroyer. Though it was not designed for the role, it was given the nickname *Zveroboy* (beast killer) for its ability to kill heavy German tanks like the Tiger and Panther. (Oliver Missing)

Red Army machine-gunner in action, winter 1944. He wears the *Telogreika* or *Vatnik*, which is a kind of warm cotton-wool-padded jacket. It was also standard winter issue on the Eastern Front. He is armed with the PPSh-41. (Johnny Shumate)

Medium Tank Company

The Soviet medium tank company consisted of three tank platoons supported by a number of technical personnel who would often ride with the battalion train most of the time. It contained 10 medium tanks with the bulk of them comprising the newer T-34-85, but older variants were also in common use. These tanks were split into a company headquarters and three tank platoons.

<u>Headquarters Section, Company HQ T-34-85</u>

1 x company commander, captain

1 x tank commander, lieutenant

1 x tank gunner, senior sergeant

1 x senior mechanic/driver, senior sergeant

1 x senior radio operator

<u>Others</u>

1 x deputy company commander for technical affairs, senior technician-lieutenant

1 x tank technician, technician-lieutenant

1 x engine technician

<u>3 x Platoons</u>

<u>Tank No. 1 T-34-85</u>

1 x platoon commander, senior lieutenant

1 x tank gunner, senior sergeant

1 x mechanic/driver, senior sergeant

1 x senior radio operator/hull machine-gunner, senior sergeant

1 x loader, sergeant

<u>Tank No. 2 T-34-85</u>

1 x tank commander, lieutenant

1 x tank gunner, senior sergeant

1 x mechanic/driver

1 x radio operator/hull machine-gunner/ deputy mechanic/driver, junior sergeant

1 x loader, sergeant

<u>Tank No. 3 T-34-85</u>

1 x tank commander, lieutenant

1 x tank gunner, senior sergeant

1 x mechanic/driver, senior sergeant

1 x radio operator/hull machine-gunner/ deputy mechanic/driver, junior sergeant

1 x loader, sergeant

Heavy Tank Company

The bulk of the heavy tank regiments were equipped with the IS-2 heavy tank during 1944. However, there were many regiments still equipped with older tanks such as the KV-1, KV-1s, KV-85, and Churchill heavy tanks. These tanks were heavily embroiled in action and fought many successful engagements. By the end of 1944 only a few regiments were left with older tank variants with many IS-2 tanks on the battlefield.

Soviet troops during one of their many assaults against Army Group North in 1943. By the summer of 1943, the German front was managing to hold.

Soviet Commanders

General Ivan Khristoforovich Bagramyan (1st Baltic Front)

Bagramyan was a competent but aggressive commander. His string of victories on the Eastern Front led him to command the 1st Baltic Front in lifting the siege of Leningrad in January 1944. Months later he commanded his Baltic Front units in Operation *Bagration* and then during the Baltic Offensive into East Prussia.

General Pyotr Malyshev (4th Shock Army)

Malyshev was regarded as innovative and independently minded. He was popular among his troops. As commander of the 4th Shock Army, in terms of his enemy, he was seen as devoid of all sentiment, and was cold-blooded and brutal in his dealings with him. He was successful in campaigns around Leningrad, against German Army Group Center, and in the Baltic Offensive.

General Ivan Khristoforovich Bagramyan with his wife, Tamara Hamayakovna.

General Pyotr Malyshev.

General Andrey Yeryomenko (2nd Baltic Army)

In April 1944, Yeryomenko was given the command of the 2nd Baltic Army. Known for his austerity and forbidding personality, as well his high moral code, this successful Eastern Front commander led his army to crush some 30 German divisions bottled up in Latvia during his aggressive drive on the capital, Riga.

Lieutenant-General Nikolai Simonyak (3rd Shock Army)

Simonyak was noted for his serious, purposeful and rational bearing. His successes in battles around Leningrad, Narva, and during the Tallinn Offensive led him to command the 3rd Shock Army, which saw him take part in the blockade of the Courland pocket. He was replaced and transferred to command the 67th Army, which was responsible for the defense of the coastline off the Gulf of Riga.

Lieutenant-General Ivan Maslennikov (3rd Baltic Army)

Maslennikov was universally respected and held somewhat in awe by his officers and troops alike. On the battlefield he was a brilliant commander and saw a string of successes on the Eastern Front when he was posted to the Leningrad Front in December 1943. From there he commanded the 3rd Baltic Army which pushed the Germans back to the Panther-Wotan Line. He remained on the Baltic Front until the end of 1944.

General Andrey Yeryomenko.

Lieutenant-General Nikolai Simonyak.

Lieutenant-General Ivan Maslennikov.

General Ivan Chernyakovskiy (3rd Belorussian Front)

As one of the heroes of the battle of Kursk in 1943, Chernyakovsky was the youngest ever Soviet army general. As commander of the 3rd Belorussian Front, he was recognized as an excellent and energetic commander that his troops looked up to. After crossing the Neman River and taking Kaunas, his army thrust forward against the eastern frontier of East Prussia. Aged 37, he was killed on February 18, 1945 by artillery fire while inspecting preparations for an offensive against Königsberg.

Lieutenant-General Porfiry Chanchibadze (2nd Guards Army)

Chanchibadze was a Stalingrad and Crimea veteran. He was regarded as a harsh general but had moral and courageous zeal which earned him respect on the battlefield. On June 4, 1944, he became commander of the 2nd Guards Army which he led with great success in the Siauliai, Memel, and East Prussia offensive operations. He also commanded the army during the assault on the fortified city of Königsberg.

Colonel-General Pavel Kurochkin (2nd Belorussian Front)

Kurochkin was a hard-headed general, but his brutal leadership on the battlefield and his talent for getting the very last ounce of strength and drop of blood from his combat divisions led to a string of successes. He took command of the 2nd Belorussian Front in February 1944, and by July he was leading a series of heavy attacks northwest of Vitebsk as part of a major Soviet offensive east of Riga, toward Rezekne, in order to cut off the German Army Group North.

General Ivan Chernyakovskiy.

Lieutenant-General Porfiry Chanchibadze.

Colonel-General Pavel Kurochkin.

GERMAN ARMY GROUP NORTH ORDER OF BATTLE, JUNE 1944

Reserves

12th Panzer Division

SIXTEENTH ARMY

Reserves

24th Infantry Division

69th Infantry Division

281st Security Division

285th Security Division

I Army Corps

205th Infantry Division

87th Infantry Division

X Army Corps

389th Infantry Division

290th Infantry Division

263rd Infantry Division

II Army Corps

81st Infantry Division

329th Infantry Division

23rd Infantry Division

VI SS Corps

15th SS Grenadier Division Latvian.1

19th SS Grenadier Division Latvian.2

93rd Infantry Division

Headquarters VI SS Corps

207th Security Division

300th Division zbV (Estonian border guard units)

L Army Corps

218th Infantry Division

132nd Infantry Division

83rd Infantry Division

18TH ARMY

Reserves

215th Infantry Division

XXXVIII Army Corps

21st Luftwaffe Field Division

32nd Infantry Division

121st Infantry Division

XXVIII Army Corps

30th Infantry Division

21st Infantry Division

212th Infantry Division

126th Infantry Division

12th Luftwaffe Field Division

1st (Estonian) Grenzschutz-Regiment

2nd & 3rd (Estonian) Grenzschutz-Regiments (attached to 227th Infantry Division)

4th (Estonian) Grenzschutz-Regiment

5th (Estonian) Grenzschutz-Regiment (attached to 207th Security Division)

207th Security Division & 5th (Estonian) Grenzschutz-Regiment

ARMY DETACHMENT NARVA

Army Reserves

61st Infantry Division

XXVI Army Corps

227th Infantry Division & 2nd & 3rd (Estonian) Grenzschutz-Regiments

170th Infantry Division

225th Infantry Division

XXXXIII Army Corps

58th Infantry Division

11th Infantry Division

122nd Infantry Division

III SS Panzer Corps

SS Panzergrenadier Division Nordland & SS Grenadier Brigade Nederland

20th SS Grenadier Division Estonian

Kustenverteidigung EAST

2nd Luftwaffe Flak Division & 5th (Estonian) Battalion

Kustenverteidigung WEST

285th Security Division & 4th (Estonian) Battalion

Military formations subordinated to Army Detachment Narva 1 March 1944:

XXVI Army Corps (General Anton Grasser)

11th Infantry Division

58th Infantry Division

214th Infantry Division

225th Infantry Division

3rd Estonian Border Guard Regiment (15 April)

XXXXIII Army Corps (General Karl von Oven)

61st Infantry Division

170th Infantry Division

227th Infantry Division

Feldherrnhalle Armored Infantry Division

Gnesen Grenadier Regiment

III SS (Germanic) Armored Corps

(SS-Obergruppenführer Felix Steiner)

11th SS Armored Grenadier Division Nordland

4th SS Armored Grenadier Brigade Nederland

20th Armed Grenadier (Infantry) Division of the (1st Estonian)

Separate Corps

Eastern Sector, Coastal Defense (Staff of 2nd Antiaircraft Division as HQ) (Lieutenant-General Alfons Luczny)

Estonian Regiment Reval

29th Estonian Police Battalion

31st Estonian Police Battalion

32nd Estonian Police Battalion

658th Eastern Battalion (Estonian)

659th Eastern Battalion (Estonian)

Other military units:

Artillery Command No. 113

High Pioneer Command No. 32

502nd Heavy Tank Battalion

752nd Antitank Battalion

540th Special Infantry (Training) Battalion

EIGHTEENTH ARMY
15 July 1944
XXVIII Army Corps

Kampfgruppe Hoefer

12th Luftwaffe Division

21st Infantry Division

30th Infantry Division

XXXVIII Army Corps

21st Luftwaffe Division

32nd Infantry Division

83rd Infantry Division

121st Infantry Division

L Army Corps

15th Waffen Grenadier Division of the SS (1st Latvian)

15th Waffen Grenadier Division of the SS (2nd Latvian)

93rd Infantry Division

126th Infantry Division

218th Infantry Division

Kampfgruppe Streckenbach

Direct controlled by by Army Headquarters

RED ARMY ORDER OF BATTLE, JUNE 1944

1ST BALTIC FRONT

4th Assault Army

83rd Rifle Corps

16th Rifle Division

119th Rifle Division

332nd Rifle Division

360th Rifle Division

6th Guards Army

2nd Guards Rifle Corps

9th Guards Rifle Division

166th Rifle Division

22nd Guards Rifle Corps

90th Guards Rifle Division

47th Guards Rifle Division

51st Guards Rifle Division

23rd Guards Rifle Corps

51st Guards Rifle Division

67th Guards Rifle Division

71st Guards Rifle Division

103rd Rifle Corps

29th Rifle Division

270th Rifle Division

Army Artillery

8th Guards Artillery Division

21st Breakthrough Artillery Division

43rd Army

1st Rifle Corps

179th Rifle Division

306th Rifle Division

60th Rifle Corps

357th Rifle Division

235th Rifle Division

334th Rifle Division

92nd Rifle Corps

145th Rifle Division

204th Rifle Division

1st Tank Corps

89th Tank Brigade

117th Tank Brigade

159th Tank Brigade

3rd Air Army

11th Fighter Aviation Corps

5th Guards Fighter Aviation Division

190th Fighter Aviation Division

(Includes independent air units)

3RD BELORUSSIAN FRONT

5th Artillery Corps

2nd Guards Breakthrough Division

20th Guards Breakthrough Division

4th Guards Gun Artillery Division

11th Guards Army
8th Guards Rifle Corps

5th Guards Rifle Division

26th Guards Rifle Division

83rd Guards Rifle Division

16th Guards Rifle Corps

1st Guards Rifle Division

11th Guards Rifle Division

31st Guards Rifle Division

36th Guards Rifle Corps

16th Guards Rifle Division

18th Guards Rifle Division

84th Guards Rifle Division

2nd Tank Corps

25th Guards Tank Brigade

26th Guards Tank Brigade

4th Guards Tank Brigade

Army Artillery

7th Guards Mortar (Multiple Rocket) Division

5th Army
45th Rifle Corps

159th Rifle Division

184th Rifle Division

338th Rifle Division

65th Rifle Corps

97th Rifle Division

144th Rifle Division

371st Rifle Division

72nd Rifle Corps

63rd Rifle Division

215th Rifle Division

277th Rifle Division

2nd Tank Brigade

153rd Tank Brigade

Army Artillery

3rd Guards Breakthrough Artillery Division

31st Army
36th Rifle Corps

173rd Rifle Division

220th Rifle Division

352nd Rifle Division

39th Army
5th Guards Rifle Corps

17th Guards Rifle Division

19th Guards Rifle Division

91st Guards Rifle Division

251st Guards Rifle Division

84th Rifle Corps

158th Rifle Division

164th Rifle Division

262nd Rifle Division

28th Tank Brigade

5th Tank Army
3rd Guards Tank Corps

3rd Guards Tank Brigade

18th Guards Tank Brigade

19th Guards Tank Brigade

3rd Guards Cavalry Corps

5th Guards Cavalry Division

6th Guards Cavalry Division

32nd Guards Cavalry Division

3rd Guards Mechanized Corps

7th Guards Mechanized Brigade

8th Guards Mechanized Brigade

35th Guards Mechanized Brigade

1st Air Army
1st Guards Bomber Corps

3rd Guards Bomber Aviation Division

4th Guards Bomber Aviation Division

5th Guards Bomber Aviation Division

6th Guards Bomber Aviation Division

113th Guards Bomber Aviation Division

334th Guards Bomber Aviation Division

213th Guards Bomber Aviation Division

(Includes Fighter Aviation Corps)

2ND BELORUSSIAN FRONT
33rd Army

70th Rifle Division

157th Rifle Division

344th Rifle Division

49th Army
62nd Rifle Corps

64th Rifle Division

330th Rifle Division

369th Rifle Division

69th Rifle Corps

42nd Rifle Division

222nd Rifle Division

76th Rifle Corps

49th Rifle Division

199th Rifle Division

290th Rifle Division

81st Rifle Corps

32nd Rifle Division

95th Rifle Division

153rd Rifle Division

42nd Guards Tank Brigade

43rd Guards Tank Brigade

50th Army
19th Rifle Corps

324th Rifle Division

362nd Rifle Division

38th Rifle Corps

110th Rifle Division

139th Rifle Division

385th Rifle Division

121st Rifle Corps

238th Rifle Division

307th Rifle Division

380th Rifle Division

(Includes the 4th Air Army)

Battle for the Narva Bridgehead

In Army Group North, General George Kuechler's force had for some weeks been trying in vain to hold positions along its northern defenses, from the Volkhov River to the Gulf of Finland, against strong Soviet forces. The Red Army's plan had been to create relentless pressure on the German lines which they believed would cause its eventual collapse. Stalin had ordered that the Red Army conduct major offensives along the entire Soviet–German front in a continuation of the "Broad Front" strategy that he had pursued since the beginning of the war in the East. He knew that Army Group North was fragile and if enough weight was applied, it would be the first of the German army groups to crack.

Red Army tank men standing next to their SU-122 assault gun in early 1944. This crew is part of the 1439th SU Regiment of the Leningrad Front. Note the two Russian soldiers wearing captured German helmets and armed with the PPSh-41 "Shpagin's" machine pistol, or commonly, the *Papasha*.

In late 1943, the Soviet winter campaign commenced, and in the northern sector of the front major assaults were unleashed around Leningrad and westward towards the region of the Baltic Sea. It was planned that Leningrad would be secured first and that the Red Army was to advance and break through the Narva Isthmus situated between the Gulf of Finland and Lake Peipus. Known as the "Estonian Operation," this was of major strategic importance to the Soviets. Its success would provide an unobstructed path in which the main Baltic Soviet armies could advance along the coast to Tallinn, forcing the German Army Group North to flee Estonia for fear of getting cut off and annihilated.

In order to avert a catastrophe unfolding in Army Group North, General Kuechler was replaced on January 9 by General Model. Hitler believed that Model would prevent the deep withdrawal of troops in the northern sector.

However, two weeks later, Model's appointment failed to prevent the city of Leningrad being liberated on January 26. As a result, the German Eighteenth Army was now split into three parts and struggled to hold any type of cohesive front forward of the Luga River. The general, determined as ever, tried to restore the disintegrating front. Both the Sixteenth and Eighteenth Armies had been drained of men and materials with only the 12th Panzer and 58th Infantry Divisions intact. These formations were ordered to hold the line at all costs on the Luga River east of a series of heavily constructed defenses which ran along the Panther-Wotan Line on the Estonian border. Model also instructed that all stragglers were to be rounded up and sent back to the line to fight. He cancelled leaves, sent walking wounded to their units, and dispatched a number of rear-echelon troops to the front. Without hesitation he requested more reinforcements, which included Waffen-SS replacements, naval coastal batteries and Luftwaffe troops.

A Red Army mortar crew during a fire mission in early 1944. Note the Soviet M-72 motorcycle. Along the German lines of Army Group North there had been barely any fighting, when out of nowhere the Volkhov and 2nd Baltic Fronts launched a massive offensive, the speed and ferocity of which took Germans by complete surprise.

The Führer
Führer Headquarters
High Command of the Army
Führer Order No. 11   8th March 1944

(Commandants of Fortified Areas and Battle Commandants) In view of various incidents, I issue the following orders:

1. A distinction will be made between "Fortified Areas," each under a "Fortified Area Commandant," and "Local Strong Points," each under a "Battle Commandant." The "Fortified Areas" will fulfill the functions of fortresses in former historical times. They will ensure that the enemy does not occupy these areas of decisive operational importance. They will allow themselves to be surrounded, thereby holding down the largest possible number of enemy forces, and establishing conditions for successful counterattacks. Local strong points deep in the battle area will be tenaciously defended in the event of enemy penetrations. By being included in the main line of battle they will act as a reserve of defense and, should the enemy break through, as hinges and cornerstones for the front, forming positions from which counterattacks can be launched.

2. Each "Fortified Area Commandant" should be a specially selected, hardened soldier, preferably of General's rank. The Army Group concerned will appoint him. Fortified Area commandants will be instructed to be personally responsible to the Commander-in-Chief of the Army Group. Fortified Area Commandants will pledge their honour as soldiers to carry out their duties to the last. Only the Commander-in-Chief of an Army Group in person may, with my approval, relieve the Fortified Area commandant of his duties, and perhaps order the surrender of the fortified area. Fortified Area Commandants are subordinate to the Commander of the Army Group, or Army, in whose sector the fortified area is situated. Further delegation of command to general officers commanding formations will not take place. Apart from the garrison and its security forces, all persons within a fortified area, or who have been collected there, are under the orders of the commandant, irrespective of whether they are soldiers or civilians, and without regard to their rank or appointment. The Fortified Area Commandant has the military rights and disciplinary powers of a commanding general. In the performance of duties, he will have at his disposal mobile courts martial and civilian courts. The Army Group concerned will appoint the staff of Fortified Area Commandants. The Chiefs of Staff will be appointed by High Command of the Army, in accordance with suggestions made by the Army Group.

3. The Garrison of a fortified area comprises: the security garrison, and the general garrison. The security garrison must be inside the fortified area at all times. Its strength will be laid down by Commander-in-Chief Army Group, and will be determined by the size of the area and the tasks to be fulfilled (preparation and completion of defenses, holding the fortified area against raids or local attacks by the enemy). The general garrison must be made available to the commandant of the fortified area in sufficient time for the men to have taken up defensive positions and be installed when a full-scale enemy attack threatens. Its strength will be laid down by the Commander-in-Chief Army Group, in accordance with the size of the fortified area and the task which is to be performed (total defense of the fortified area).

Signed: ADOLF HITLER

In Profile:

German SdKfz.234/4 Reconnaissance Vehicle and Sd.Kfz.251/9 Personnel Carrier

This Sd.Kfz.234/4 reconnaissance vehicle is armed with a 7.5cm PaK 40 and for local defense mounts an MG 42. It has received a coat of white winter camouflage paint applied over the dark sand base, covering all the markings. (Oliver Missing)

This Sd.Kfz.251/9 halftrack operating in Lithuania is armed with the 7.5cm L/24 low-velocity gun and is equipped for local defense with the MG 42. The vehicle is painted in dark sand with a camouflage scheme of brown patches sprayed over the whole vehicle. Foliage has been applied over parts of the halftrack for additional camouflage protection. (Oliver Missing)

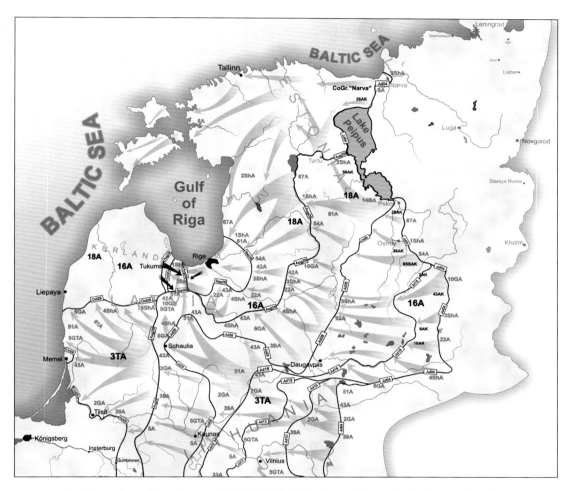

Red Army front lines January 1–March 30, 1944. Soviet forces had advanced as far as the city of Narva, southward to Lake Peipus and down to Ostroy-Konez, stretching in a southerly direction through Estonia.

Over the coming weeks Soviet forces of the Volkhov and Leningrad Fronts began exerting more pressure, especially against the Sixteenth Army that was defending positions along the Baltic. But thankfully for the Germans, the spring thaw arrived early and melting snow turned the roads into quagmires. It seemed the front was temporarily holding, with the weather playing a major part in containing the Red Army. In order to instill further determination into the troops to defend their positions to the bitter end, Hitler sent his "Fortified Area" order to his front-line commanders (see box inset).

Two photographs taken in sequence showing winter-clad German soldiers preparing their Panzerwerfer 42 auf Maultier (Sd.Kfz.4/1) for a fire mission in Army Group North. Mounting the 15cm Panzerwerfer, these weapons were used for larger-scale rocket barrages against Soviet positions where a large bombardment of a wider area would be more effective than more accurate artillery fire.

The Soviets were determined in early 1944 to capitalize on their successful Leningrad–Novgorod offensive with the main intention of reconquering Estonia. The Baltic Sea seemed the most direct and quickest way for the Red Army to take control of the German war machine in the north and seize the Baltic states. The Narva River, which stretches from Lake Peipus northward to the Gulf of Finland, had not initially been part of the Soviet plan, but German forces had fought a rearguard action until they reached the eastern bank of the Narva. Here they strengthened both the river line and the town of Narva itself, which drew considerable attention from the Red Army.

The terrain on which the Soviets would advance from Lake Peipus to the coast was low-lying, which made it ideal tank country. Much of the land was forested with swamps, cut by various waterways and vast sprawling fields. For the Germans this made for a great natural obstacle and Model was quick to employ large amounts of men and armor to defend it. He was aware that if the Narva bridgehead was broken by the Soviets, it would act as a springboard into Estonia where their powerful forces could spread across the wastelands towards Latvia and Lithuania. In order to defend Narva at all costs a formation was put together known as "Detachment Narva." The commander put in charge of it was SS-Obergruppenführer Felix Steiner. His detachment comprised the III SS (Germanic) Panzer Corps which contained mostly SS volunteer formations like Nordland, Nederland, and Estonian. There were even Estonian police battalions drafted into the defense and supported by the 502nd Heavy Tank Battalion. Narva would be later known as the "battle of the European SS."

The Narva defensive line ran for several miles from the estate of Lilienbach, northeast from the highway bridge over Narva River to the settlement of Dolgaya Niva. The 4th SS Panzergrenadier Brigade Nederland was charged with defending the northern half of the bridgehead, while the 11th SS Division Nordland held the southern flank. Attacking them along the highway and railway were the four Soviet divisions of the 43rd and 109th Rifle Corps. In spite of the fact that many of the foreign recruits were totally unsuited for combat, the Nederland Brigade and the 1st Battalion of the SS Volunteer Panzergrenadier Regiment 24 Danmark, supported by heavy German artillery, inflicted heavy casualties on the Red Army, which stalled their attack.

In other areas of the Narva front Estonian SS formations needed desperate support as their lines were cracking under Soviet pressure. In fact, the Soviet Leningrad Front had only

A winter-clad tank crew pose for the camera on board their vehicle. Within days of the Russian winter offensive in January 1944, the German front began collapsing. East of Oranienbaum and west of Leningrad the German front quickly caved in. The same happened at Novgorod where a number of German units were encircled. The Soviet 2nd Shock and 42nd Armies then joined the attack against Army Group North. (Michael Cremin)

Red Army troops on the offensive in early 1944. Note the soldier armed with the antiquated PTRD-41 "Degtyaryov" single-shot antitank weapon system model of 1941, still effective against German halftracks and lighter armored vehicles.

initially deployed vanguard elements to attack. Even the battered 58th Infantry Division, which was quickly dispatched from the Eighteenth Army and transferred north of Narva to support the Estonians, struggled to contain the Soviet forces.

The German situation was made worse when the Leningrad Front ordered the 2nd Shock Army to break through the German defensive line north and south of Narva town. Its objective was to push the front 40 miles westward and continue toward the town of Rakvere.

Three German infantrymen pose for the camera during a pause in their withdrawal across the Baltics. Along the Baltic coast some German units managed to escape as they withdrew to Estonia, but many were trapped and destroyed as the Soviets swept in from the east and west. At Novgorod eight Soviet divisions encircled five German battalions. Their one hope to escape annihilation was by hiding in the swamps west of the city. (Michael Cremin)

On February 11, massed artillery of the 2nd Shock Army opened fire on all German positions. The 30th Guards Rifle Corps, an elite unit usually used in breaching defensive lines, joined the Soviet units and stormed the German positions. Guards riflemen then wrenched open a gap in the Narva bridgehead several miles wide. As a result, remnants of the German 227th and 170th Divisions retreated.

The situation for the Germans along the Narva bridgehead was turning into a disaster. The Leningrad Front was now putting considerable effort into crushing enemy defenses along the frontier of Estonia and formed two bridgeheads north and south of the Tallinn highway. Detachment Narva was struggling under systemic artillery bombardments and infantry and armored assaults. The situation became so bad that its units were in danger of being encircled and besieged. In front of Narva the highway was held by a motley collection of infantry units formed from field divisions of the Luftwaffe and supported by Panther and Tiger tanks that were positioned every few hundred yards along the highway. Yet, in spite of this defense, Soviet artillery kept the highway under constant bombardment.

Conditions for the German soldiers and their foreign volunteers were becoming dire. This was made worse on February 14 when Russian naval troops of the 260th Independent Naval Infantry Brigade landed several gunboats on the coast northwest of Narva, known as the *Meerapalu* landing operation. In order to meet this threat the 1st Battalion, Waffen-SS Grenadier Regiment 45 Estland and an East Prussian battalion of the 44th Grenadier Regiment defended the coastal region, thwarting the Soviet attack.

A German 15cm gun crew during a fire mission on the Narva front. The Red Army winter offensive was so swift that in January and February 1944 the Leningrad Front had reached the borders of Estonia. However, Hitler prohibited all voluntary withdrawal, reserving all decisions to withdraw for himself. As a result of this order, the Leningrad Front's offensive towards the Estonian capital Tallinn was halted by strong German resistance in February. The Eighteenth Army alone though incurred more than 50,000 casualties.

SS motorcyclists on the Narva front. By February 2, 1944, the Red Army was bearing down along the frontier of Estonia and threatening the city of Narva. The Germans had already established a large and strongly defended bridgehead covering territory on the eastern approaches to Narva. Soldiers from the SS Division Nordland and Brigade Nederland were well dug in and all available reserves were rushed to the front lines, which included the release of an Estonian brigade.

Elsewhere along the front the Germans continued to resist at all costs as mounting pressure on their lines was causing considerable problems, with the Red Army increasing the intensity of their attacks. Although lines of trenches were dug, reinforced with machine-gun and mortar pits, along with mines and extensive barbed-wire barriers and antitank guns, it was still inadequate to deal with the growing might of the Soviets.

Panzergrenadiers use an advancing Tiger tank as cover on the Narva front, February 1944. In spite of dogged resistance by both German and Estonian troops attached to SS-Obergruppenführer Felix Steiner's III SS Panzer Corps defending the Narva bridgehead, they struggled to hold the line.

In early March Soviet units began directing strong infantry and armored assaults against the town of Narva on the main road to Tallinn. A heavy Soviet air attack blew the main bridge and the baroque-style old town was destroyed by 200 aircraft dropping 3,600 bombs, with barely any buildings left intact. Only the town hall and Hermann Castle were left standing. On the morning of March 8, the Soviet air force and the artillery of the 2nd Shock Army fired 100,000 shells and grenades at the three weakened German regiments defending the town. The operation continued with the assault of the 30th Guards Rifle Division and numerous tanks, focusing on the 4th SS Volunteer Panzergrenadier Brigade Nederland. Fighting raged for the next few days which led to a sustained assault in the ruins of Lilienbach estate just northeast of Narva. The battered lines were held by units of the SS Freiwilligen Panzergrenadier Regiment 49 De Ruyter. Soon brutal fighting broke out across the defensive lines between the SS regiment and Red Army troops of the 30th Guard Rifle Corps. However, after several hours of battle, much of it hand-to-hand combat, the Russian troops were beaten back and their focus of effort shifted north of Narva.

It was here in the north that three divisions of the Soviet 14th Rifle Corps attacked defensive positions manned by the 20th Estonian SS Volunteer Division. Poorly armed and undertrained, these soldiers were slowly driven from their meagre defensive positions. Loudspeakers were set up calling on the Estonians to swap sides and join the "Soviet crusade against Nazism." However, when the defenders refused to budge, the Russians ordered in their flamethrowers to burn them out. Soviet formations then proceeded to overrun the

enemy positions and establish a bridgehead on the west bank of the river north of Narva. Here, supported by the artillery from the III Germanic Armored Corps, Estonian machine-gunners were frantically placed along the riverbank where they successfully held back three Soviet rifle divisions.

As the Soviet ground offensive gained momentum, in the air long-range bombers began bombing the key Estonian towns of Tartu, Petseri, and the capital, Tallinn. The inhabitants paid a heavy price with hundreds of civilians killed and and 20,000 made homeless.

The Narva front comprised a number of fortified areas which included bunkers and various underground encampments. Here an SS soldier is emerging from a shelter which the Germans called *Halbgruppenunterstande* (group and half-group living bunkers).

Estonian SS troops in a defensive position on the Narva bridgehead. As Red Army forces approached the borders of Estonia, a general mobilization was announced in the country by the German authorities calling on all Estonian men to volunteer and take up arms against the Red Army. Within weeks some 30,000 men had reluctantly volunteered in the Estonian Waffen-SS. The new 20th SS Division then received additional reinforcements, bringing the total of Estonian units up to 50,000–60,000 men.

A Soviet battery of 76mm guns opens up against German positions along the frontier of Estonia, March 1944.

On the ground the German front began to weaken as the Soviet 2nd Baltic Front launched a series of systematic attacks against the Sixteenth Army. Along parts of the front the Germans and their foreign conscripts continued to fight a frenzied battle of attrition. North and south of Narva fighting had been predominantly fierce and in some areas along the battered German front troops were almost encircled and close to annihilation. In spite of orders from their commanders that the defensive lines ought never be abandoned, what remained of the infantry divisions began evacuating in order to save themselves from complete annihilation. Luckily for the Germans the weather turned for the worse. Following a warm winter, the spring thaw had set in early. A foot of water covered the ice on the surrounding lakes and turned roads into a quagmire. As a result, Soviet armor halted or slowed.

By the last week of March 1944, as the German formations regrouped and prepared their defensive positions, General George Lindemann replaced Model as acting commander of Army Group North. Lindemann was no defensive expert, but he excelled as a tactician and through his daring attitude he was able to temporarily stabilize the front. As the Russians stalled along the borders of Estonia, regrouping after a number of weeks of continuous fighting, Lindemann was able to further exploit the situation and go over to the offensive. Early on March 26, the 11th, 170th, and the 227th Infantry Divisions attacked the Soviet 109th Rifle Corps in order to destroy positions on the Kriivasoo bridgehead. Grenadiers supported by Tiger and Panther tanks moved forward through the swamps and soon penetrated the fortified Soviet positions. Although the Germans were poorly matched in terms of equipment and supply, a number of grenadiers were hardened veterans that

SS foreign conscripts wearing their winter whites in a trench on the Narva front. Note their commander, ranked as an *SS-Hauptscharfuhrer*, with a pair of Zeiss binoculars.

In Profile:

Waffen-SS Sturmmann and Wehrmacht Grenadiers in Action

This Waffen-SS Sturmmann belonging to Brigade Langemarck in the winter of 1944 is well armed considering that weapons issued to foreign conscripts were at a premium. He is well kitted out too and wears the winter camouflage smock and carries two three-pocket pouches holding 30-round magazines for his new 7.9mm StG44 assault rifle. (Johnny Shumate)

Wehrmacht soldiers in action during defensive operations in Latvia. The soldier armed with a Karbiner 98K bolt action rifle wears the green splinter pattern army camouflage smock, whilst his comrade armed with the StG44 assault rifle is dressed in the familiar winter white reversible jacket white side out. (Johnny Shumate)

Troops of 11th SS Panzergrenadier Division Nordland interrogate captured Russian soldiers along the Narva front, spring 1944.

An SS Langemarck PaK crew preparing their weapon for a defensive action. The main Waffen-SS force defending Estonia was SS-Grupppenführer Felix Steiner's III Germanic Panzer Corps that comprised the 11th SS Freiwilligen (Volunteer) Division Nordland and SS Freiwilligen Brigade Nederland. In addition, were the 15th and 19th Waffen Grenadier Divisions from Estonia, as well as the Flemish Langemarck Brigade and the Walloon Sturmbrigade Wallonien.

Two SS Langemarck commanders chatting in an Estonian village in the winter of 1944. In order to defend Estonia Waffen-SS units, including 24 volunteer infantry battalions from the SS Division Nordland, the SS Division Langemarck, the SS Division Nederland, and the Walloon Legion, supported the main defensive effort.

had survived some of the costliest battles in the East. Hurriedly these troops, armed with a motley assortment of antitank and flak guns, machine guns, Panzerfaust and the deadly Panzerschrek, advanced along the main roads, through the surrounding forests and swamps. When they met heavy resistance, German machine-gun platoons and antitank units dug in and held each end of the line whilst armored vehicles moved forward taking key positions and blasting Soviet emplacements.

By the end of March, in spite of determined German efforts to destroy the Kriivasoo bridgehead, the spring thaw prevented them securing the region. As a consequence, the offensive ground to a halt and German armor was reluctantly withdrawn from the most flooded areas. The front then stagnated for a several weeks whilst both sides took stock.

Soldiers of the Flemish Langemarck Brigade in a trench during defensive operations in Estonia. Though there were isolated successes where SS troops drove Red Army units back and restored their line, the Red Army force was overwhelming.

| Fall of Fortress Vilnius

Throughout April, May, and June 1944, the Narva front continued to hold as Soviet forces built up their reserves for a new offensive. The 502nd Heavy Panzer Battalion was still in the process of reinforcing the front with the 11th SS Nordland Division. The well-decorated Eastern Front Tiger tank commander Leutnant Otto Carius and his 2nd Heavy Panzer Company were quickly transferred to the Latvian town of Dünaburg to defend positions against vigorous Red Army attacks.

In anticipation of another Soviet attack along the whole northern front, Model's replacement, General Lindmann, requested additional reinforcements to the area in order to try and strengthen his lines of defense. Although a temporary lull along certain sectors had given Lindmann's divisions time to build a number of defensive positions along the front, Army Group North was totally exposed. Behind the lines the Soviet air force was continuing to bomb the rear areas including supply dumps, and reports confirmed by German commanders in the field were that the Russians were softening up targets for a ground offensive into Estonia.

However, unbeknown to the Germans, the Red Army had actually misled German intelligence regarding the presence and disposition of its forces. Through German Army Group Center, the Soviets had used a large-scale deception plan, fooling the Germans into believing they were actually going to attack in the south, when their main objective was the center.

As a consequence, Hitler ordered that vital equipment and resources be stripped from Army Group Center to create a reserve to strike a pre-emptive blow in northern Ukraine. The result meant that most of its panzers, a quarter of its self-propelled guns, half its antitank capability, and over a quarter of its heavy artillery were removed from Army Group Center and transported south.

In Army Group North Lindmann believed that the Soviet Baltic Front had temporarily halted its attack into the Baltic states due to the imminent offensive in northern Ukraine. However, by early June, German intelligence began receiving disturbing reports that Soviet armor was moving north. By the first week of June there were strong indications that Red Army infantry divisions and artillery were concentrating opposite Army Group Center. Days later reports confirmed that four Soviet armies had been detected facing the army group.

On June 19, a final report indicated that a huge Soviet offensive was poised to be launched against Army Group Center, its codename Operation *Bagration*. Three days later the offensive was unleashed in which Army Group Center was compelled to attempt to counter. The Soviet attack was swift, deep, wide and bloody, which resulted in a catastrophe of unbelievable proportions for the Germans. Although many German units continued to fight a grim and bitter defense, the Red Army had already punched through the lines,

Two images taken in sequence showing the Nebelwerfer during a nighttime fire mission against an enemy target. These Nebelwerfer rocket barrages covered much larger areas than standard artillery but added more of a psychological element to the battlefield, especially at night. Noise, smoke, and flying debris as the rockets impacted and exploded were considerable.

allowing an almost seemingly unstoppable flood of infantry and armor encircling precious German panzer and infantry divisions. The reverberations caused by the offensive were immense and even Army Group North felt the shockwaves. With the situation increasingly worsening and concerns over the prospect of Army Group Center completely collapsing, Army Group North was ordered to establish contact with the left flank of the Third Panzer Army. Although the plan seemed as if it might stabilize the northern sector of Army Group Center, it took vulnerable units away from the Baltic states which were already experiencing Red Army attacks along their lines. Consequently, Army Group North became totally exposed by the *Bagration* offensive. The entire region was thrown into complete chaos.

Two photographs taken in sequence showing winter-clad soldiers of the 15th Latvian SS Grenadier Division during a lull in the fighting sharing a carafe (probably of wine). Much of the division was trapped in the chaos of the collapse of the Army Group North front. This division had seen heavy fighting in the Ostrov, Novosokolniki, and Novgorod Oblasts of Leningrad.

Hitler ordered that Lindmann immediately draw off more units from Army Group North and launch a counterattack in order to prop up the Third Panzer Army. When the general was unable to launch the counterattack, Hitler sacked him on July 4, and replaced him with General Johannes Friessner. In Hitler's eyes Friessner had distinguished himself as a commander of Army Detachment Narva.

When Friessner arrived at army group headquarters at Segewold, he held a conference with his field commanders, displaying confidence in stabilizing the front. Yet, he had taken over an arena of operations that was on the verge of destruction. His forces were outnumbered

In Profile:

Tiger Tank "217" at Malinava and Soviet IS-2, 48th Heavy Tank Regiment, 2nd Baltic Front

A mid-production Tiger I tank, "217" belonged to Otto Carius, 2./sPzAbt.502, at the time of the battle at Malinava in Latvia in July 1944. It is painted in overall dark sand with a very light pattern of green patches. (Oliver Missing)

This is one of the five IS-2 tanks destroyed at Malinava by Tiger "217" of 2./sPzAbt.502. (Oliver Missing)

eight to one, and due to the swift success of the *Bagration* offensive, by early July, the 1st Baltic Front was now racing towards Baranovichi and Molodechno and reaching the Latvian and Lithuanian frontiers. Along these borders were numerous German strongholds, but with no reserves behind them to prevent the Red Army from driving to the Baltic coast.

In spite of this dire situation, every unit in Army Group North was ordered to halt and prepare to launch a counterattack in order to regain contact with the Third Panzer Army. Friessner ordered that two infantry divisions be withdrawn from the Eighteenth Army to support units in Army Group Center. This, once again, saw Army Group North become even more susceptible to Soviet attack. On July 9, eight Soviet rifle divisions pushed back I Corps, while the 6th Soviet Guards Army drove into Latvia opposed only by three construction engineer battalions and some ad hoc Latvian police units.

The main objective of the Red Army was to capture the town of Molodechno and then thrust onto Vilnius, the capital of Lithuania. Due to the *Bagration* offensive the Red Army had sent Army Group Center reeling back in disarray westward and northward. As they withdrew some German units poured across into Lithuania with Red Army forces in pursuit, smashing holes along the borders and penetrating deep into the country.

With the Russian advance into Lithuania, the commander of the Sixteenth Army, General Christian Hansen, was openly blamed by an enraged Hitler. He was replaced by the highly competent General Paul Laux. Within days of taking command, Laux was put to the test as General Eremenko's 2nd Baltic Front launched a major offensive against the

The mid-production Tiger I tank, "217," belonging to Otto Carius, 2./sPzAbt.502. By the summer Carius's 2nd Company had been deployed to Latvia and took part in defensive actions at Malinava.

Belonging to the Flemish Langemarck Brigade, an 8cm Granatwerfer 34 mortar during a fire mission.

left flank of the Sixteenth Army, which was defended by the German VI SS Corps and X Corps. The divisions that bore the brunt of the attack were the 15th SS and 19th SS Latvian Divisions, the 93rd Infantry, 23rd Infantry, 329th Infantry, 281st Security, and the 263rd Infantry Divisions.

The Soviet attack against the Sixteenth Army was heavy, and, in spite of sustaining considerable casualties, they could rely on substantial support and reinforcements. The Soviet 6th Guards Army in the Baltic Gap, along with the 2nd Guards Army and 31st Army, which were advancing into eastern Lithuania, moved up to support the offensive and apply further pressure on the German and Latvian divisions.

On July 14, to make matters worse, the 3rd Baltic Front then joined the offensive, smashing into the right wing of the Eighteenth Army. Its objective was to separate the Sixteenth and Eighteenth Armies. Already Army Group North was struggling to maintain any type of cohesion against the might of the Soviet

Russian soldiers of the Leningrad Front in a trench prior to going into action. Note the Degtyaryov machine gun, or DP-27, propped up against the trench wall.

Baltic Front. It was estimated that since the Red Army had unleashed *Bagration*, Army Group North had suffered some 50,000 casualties, and it was reckoned that only two of the Sixteenth Army's divisions, the 61st and 225th Infantry, were fully combat effective.

In a measure to try and stabilize the deteriorating situation, Friessner journeyed to Hitler's East Prussian headquarters, Wolfsschanze, the Wolf's Lair. Here he discussed with the Führer plans of withdrawing his forces to the Duena River. Hitler, however, forbade any type of tactical withdrawal from the battlefront. Instead, he astonished Friessner by telling him that his forces should launch a counterattack in order to restore contact with Army Group Center. With no reinforcements available, Hitler said, if necessary, Army Detachment Narva was to be stripped of its units and sent to assist in the counterattack. By undertaking this action, Friessner said, it would see the collapse of the Narva front and allow Soviet troops to pour into Estonia and secure Tallinn. Hitler obstinately retorted, telling his general that Army Group Center was to be stabilized or the whole front in the region would collapse.

Meanwhile, back at the front, Army Group North's situation continued to worsen. Fighting was bitter and the German divisions simply had too much of an extended front to be able to defend it for any appreciable length of time. Yet, in spite of the overwhelming might of the enemy, towns and villages were fanatically defended, with all and any available armor often brought in to stem the Soviet onslaught. At the village of Malinava, a suburb in northern Dünaburg, Otto Carius with his 2nd Company of the 502nd Heavy Tank Battalion of eight Tigers were ordered to stop the Soviet attacks. Carius recalls that the entire battle

Three Soviet ISU-122s advance. ISU-122s were often fielded in mixed units with the ISU-152, and used as an assault gun, a self-propelled howitzer, or a long-range tank destroyer.

did not last more than 20 minutes: he used only two of his Tigers to knock out 17 of the new JS-1 Stalin and five T-34 tanks. He then brought up the rest of his company of six Tigers to ambush the remainder of the Soviet tank battalion advancing toward him. As a result, a further 28 tanks were destroyed along with their supporting trucks and vehicles: the complete Soviet battalion had been destroyed with no loss to Carius's Tigers.

In spite of a number of defensive successes by the Germans, these measures were often isolated and had no real military impact on the overall Red Army offensive. Both Latvia and Lithuania were now totally exposed to the Russian onslaught. In Lithuania the Soviets stormed the frontier following the success of the *Bagration*, and had annihilated withdrawing German formations. As a result, the Lithuanian capital, Vilnius, was now threatened. The city was subjected to Hitler's "Fortified Area" order, and commanders had been ordered that it must be held at all costs. Hitler was hoping to defend the city with four panzer divisions, but was told these could not be assembled before July 23. It was imperative to hold Vilnius, he said, because without it, the Red Army would use the city as a springboard to carve its way through Lithuania along the Baltic coast westward into East Prussia. Without Vilnius he was concerned that it would be almost impossible to re-establish a sustainable connection between Army Group North and Army Group Center.

A StuG. III withdrawing to a new defensive line in the summer of 1944. With the annihilation of Army Group Center much of the pressure now fell on Army Group North. In order to avert a catastrophe a new defensive line was implemented—the Tannenberg Line (Tannenbergstellung)—with the main defenses erected to the west of Narva. On July 21, Hitler grudgingly ordered a general withdrawal to the Tannenberg Line, and to fight to the death there.

Red Army troops reach the Polish border in July 1944, having utterly crushed Army Group Center during the *Bagration* summer offensive.

For this reason, Vilnius had become known as "Fortress Vilnius." It was under the command of Luftwaffe General Rainer Stahel, and elements of the Third Panzer Army under the command of General Georg-Hans Reinhardt. The garrison was comprised of a battalion from the 16th Parachute (Fallschirmjäger) Regiment, the 399th Grenadier Regiment, 1067th Grenadier Regiment, 240th Artillery Regiment of the 170th Infantry Division, an antitank battalion of the 256th Infantry Division, and various other random units.

Over the next few days Fortress Vilnius tried to hold out against heavy attacks by the 5th Guards Tank Army. In spite of heavy combat formations of 8.8cm Flak guns, committed to the battle against armored attacks, the defense weakened and the city was on the point of capitulating. General Stahel realized that his fortress would soon be surrounded. During the night of July 12/13, after destroying all their heavy weapons, most of the German troops broke out of the city in a westerly direction. Almost 3,000 grenadiers left the decimated city, with many frantically swimming the river to reach lead elements of the 6th Panzer Division.

In spite of fanatical resistance by what was left of the German garrison, the Soviets managed to split the garrison into two pockets, thus sealing the fate of the defenders trapped inside. In quick order the defense totally collapsed, leaving thousands of German troops killed and wounded. On the evening of July 13, the garrison finally surrendered.

After the fall of Vilnius, fighting in the area continued with unabated ferocity. The 6th Panzer Division fought to open a route through to Zysmory, whilst remnants of the IX Army Corps were embroiled in bitter fighting near Anyksciai. Losses were terrible.

It appeared that the defense of Lithuania was now under serious threat of collapse. In spite of constant appeals from Army Group Center for assistance, Army Group North could not release any of its divisions for they were already fighting for their survival against the massed attacks of the 2nd and 3rd Baltic Fronts.

By late July the entire army group was in full retreat except Army Detachment Narva, which was still fanatically resisting on the far-left flank of the Eighteenth Army. The position for Army Group North deteriorated further as Soviet forces advanced deeper into Lithuania and Latvia. Around the Latvian city of Dünaburg heavy fighting had been raging day and night for almost a week. Remnants of the German 393rd Assault Gun Brigade had lost all its guns in the fighting, and the 502nd Panzer Division was totally destroyed. When the smouldering city was eventually surrounded, the army group ordered it be abandoned. Frantically Friessner radioed the Führer's headquarters, appealing to Hitler for a general retreat.

As a result of Friessner's persistent demands, he was relieved of his command forthwith and dispatched to command Army Group South Ukraine. He was replaced by one of Hitler's most brutal field commanders, General Ferdinand Schörner, who was universally despised by his troops. He considered the Russian population to be subhuman and his Führer looked at him to be able to stabilize the front knowing that his fanatical Nazi beliefs would bring about success.

German troops surrender to the Red Army in Vilnius, the Lithuanian capital.

Red Army troops listen in intently at a briefing, along the Narva front in the summer of 1944.

Estonia Buckles

When General Schörner took command of the Baltic operations, Army Group North had a total combat strength of some 700,000 men. Seven of its divisions were fully combat effective: the 11th, 21st, 30th, 58th, 61st, and 227th Infantry Divisions, and the 12th Luftwaffe Field Division. The rest, including the 15th and 19th Latvian SS Divisions, were totally exhausted and ineffective.

Against Schörner's army stood the Soviet 2nd Baltic, 3rd Baltic, and Leningrad Fronts. Some 12 armies with more than 80 divisions were distributed between these fronts. The main focus of attention now that Vilnius had been captured was Tallinn. However, before the Estonian capital could be taken, the town of Narva needed to be seized.

Russian POWs captured during the battle of Narva have been rounded up and are awaiting their fate.

At a forward observation post a German soldier surveys the Narva front during operations in July 1944. The battle for the Narva bridgehead had raged since early February. (Michael Cremin)

Narva was still being defended by Felix Steiner's III SS Panzer Corps, which consisted of European volunteers of Dutch, Flemish, Walloon, Norwegian, Swede, Danish, and German extraction. The veteran East Prussian 11th Infantry Division had been added, including the undertrained and under-armed 4th and 6th Estonian Border Guards Regiments. Steiner knew there were insufficient forces to defend Narva. In order to prevent the wholesale destruction of his army detachment, he began preparations for a withdrawal to the Tannenberg Line (Tannenbergstellung) in the Sinimäed hills, 10 miles from Narva. The commanders of the Soviet Leningrad Front were

A column of Soviet T-34 tanks deploys to the Narva bridgehead.

unaware of the preparations. Instead, they were preparing a fresh Narva offensive with shock troops from the Finnish front who had taken up positions near the town. This gave the Leningrad Front a four-to-one superiority both in manpower and equipment. However, just as Steiner implemented his withdrawal order, the Soviet 8th Army launched their offensive, on July 24. Some 1,360 assault guns and hundreds of tanks supported the Soviet attack. As Russian troops began crossing the river north of the city, the 2nd Battalion, 1st Estonian Regiment kept the Soviet shock army from capturing the highway as Steiner's troops began withdrawing. Some 113 Soviet tanks were destroyed, many knocked out by the deadly Panzerfaust and well-positioned antitank guns. Once the withdrawal had been successfully undertaken, the last of the defenders were either killed, captured, or clawed their way back onto the highway to join the remainder of Steiner's corps. The Soviets finally captured Narva on July 26 after six long months of German defense.

The bulk of the German forces then fell back to the Tannenberg Line. Here Steiner's corps dug in, along with his foreign volunteers. The Russians were determined to smash the Tannenberg Line as they considered it the key objective for an advance along the Baltic to reach East Prussia. For the attack the 2nd Shock Army was to break through the defensive line of the III SS Panzer Corps at Orphanage Hill, wrench open the enemy's lines, destroy his communications and advance west, and supported by heavy air assaults, to reach the Kunda River. The Soviets brought up 11 divisions and six tank regiments, including the new IS-2 tanks, all supported by reinforcements and fresh manpower. In total the Leningrad Front comprised 54,850 troops, 976 artillery piece, 286 tanks, and 44 self-propelled guns. In front of the Soviet force stood a number of battered and worn-out German regiments with no reserves. They had suffered for weeks from constant Soviet artillery bombardments, and were exhausted. In total 22,250 troops were deployed in 25 Estonian and 24 German, Dutch, Danish, Flemish, Italian, Norwegian, and Walloon battalions.

A Soviet SU-152 attached to the Baltic Front advances through an Estonian forest in the summer of 1944. These tanks assumed an adopted role as heavy tank destroyers and were more than capable of knocking out the heaviest German armored vehicles such as the Tiger and Panther, and even the Elefant tank destroyers.

In Profile:
Soviet SU-152 Tank and STZ-5 Rocket Launcher, Baltic Front

An SU-152 advancing toward the front through Estonia in the summer of 1944. The vehicle is painted in overall dark green and displays the tactical number "200" which is painted in white on the hull side. (Oliver Missing)

A stationary Soviet US6-based BM-13N Katyusha multiple rocket launcher. The design of these mobile rocket launchers comprised racks of parallel rails on which rockets were mounted, with a folding frame to raise the rails to launch position. Each truck had 14 to 48 launchers. These weapons were used extensively on the Eastern Front and were much feared by the Germans. (Oliver Missing)

Foreign Waffen-SS troops along the Narva front survey a bomb crater. In the distance is a knocked-out T-34.

Very young European volunteers from Felix Steiner's III SS Panzer Corps in a jovial mood.

A typical defensive position along the Narva front. Here an SS heavy MG 34 machine gun position can be seen waiting for an enemy assault. (Michael Cremin)

A Soviet 120mm mortar crew in action, as a female soldier bandages a soldier's head wound.

A flak crew from the 2nd Battalion, Narva Brigade Langemarck.

The main Soviet attack was against the Sinimäed region which began with an overwhelming frontal assault on July 29. All along the battered Tannenberg Line German troops and their foreign counterparts tried in vain to hold their positions against overwhelming odds. Whilst a number of areas simply cracked under the sheer weight of the Red Army onslaught, there were many units which continued to demonstrate their ability to defend the most hazardous positions against a well-prepared and highly superior enemy. However, by noon on July 29, Soviet forces had virtually seized control of the Tannenberg

An MG 42 crew in action defending the Narva perimeter.

A staged Soviet propaganda photograph shows Soviet troops following the capture of Narva on July 26, after six long months of dogged German defense.

The crew of a Soviet ISU-152 next to their tank destroyer during their advance through Estonia in late July 1944.

Boyish troops of the 11th SS Volunteer Panzergrenadier Division Nordland near Ivangorod. The netting over their headgear is to combat the mosquitoes that plagued the lakes and swamps during summer.

Nordland Division troops in a trench with a mortar tube.

Soviet infantry and a T-34 on the offensive in the Sinimäed hills.

Waffen-SS troops take cover on the side of a road following their withdrawal to the Tannenberg Line. A machine-gunner with his MG 34, bipod extended, is in the foreground.

A column of T-34 tanks halted in an Estonian forest during the advance on Tallinn in the summer of 1944.

89

An SU-152 and a Valentine tank pick their way through a thick forest, July 1944. This armored unit belongs to the 2nd Baltic Front, which took part in the Rezhitsa–Dvinsk offensive that advanced some 150 miles to the west.

A Soviet mortar crew prepare their 120mm mortar during a fire mission.

Line. Some German units counterattacked the Soviets besieging some of the hills in the region; the fighting was savage, resulting in terrible casualties on both sides. In Steiner's memoirs, the strength of the fire and the nature of the battles reminded him of Verdun. All along the front small German grenadier units counterattacked, moving through trenches and shell holes, and when they ran out of ammunition, they utilized Soviet grenades and automatic weapons taken from the dead.

Yet, in spite of the overwhelming attack, it appeared that the Soviets had underestimated the strength of the German defenses and their resourcefulness in counterattacking. Over the next days and weeks that followed, the Germans continued to hold their lines in spite of incurring 10,000 casualties. However, although the Tannenberg Line remained intact in a number of places, Estonia was, to all intents and purposes, lost. Many pockets of German troops remained, bypassed—but not forgotten—by the Soviets who were now preparing their decisive Baltic Offensive.

Red Army troops on the march through Estonia.

The Soviet Baltic Offensive

The Baltic Offensive, in common with other Soviet strategic offensives, covered the major frontal offensive as well as several localized individual operations. The fresh Red Army operation included the Riga Offensive, which was to be carried out by the 2nd and 3rd Baltic Fronts: the objective was to clear enemy positions along the eastern coast to the Gulf of Riga.

To coincide with this attack, the Red Army would also launch the Tallinn Offensive which was to be carried out by the Leningrad Front in order to drive out the last German formations from mainland Estonia. Once these two strategic offensives had launched, the Soviets would open the *Moonsund* landing operation, a large-scale amphibious landing on the Estonian islands of Hiiumaa, Saaremaa, and Muhu, to block escaping German units from having access to the Gulf of Riga. The final part of the operation was the Memel Offensive, which was an attack planned by the 1st Baltic Front aimed at severing the connection between German Army Groups Center and North.

On September 14, the Baltic Offensive began in earnest and, as planned, commenced with the Riga Offensive which launched the 1st, 2nd, and 3rd Baltic Fronts; their objective was to capture the Latvian capital of Riga and cut off Army Group North in Courland in western Latvia and the Gulf of Riga. This forced the III SS Panzer Corps to finally withdraw

A Soviet mortar crew rush across an open field during an attack on a position in Latvia.

from the Tannenberg Line and link up with units of Army Group North in their retreat. As the Soviets advanced on September 17, the 3rd Baltic Front opened the Tallinn Offensive from the Emajogi River front, which joined Lake Peipus with Lake Vortsjarv. The main Soviet objective of the offensive was to attack and encircle Army Detachment Narva. The offensive was swift, but by almost superhuman effort and with some courageous fighting the Germans managed to temporarily slow the Soviet advance while their depleted formations withdrew to the Latvian border.

In Estonia the military situation worsened. General Schörner decided to evacuate his forces from the country before they were driven along the Baltic coast and cut off. The withdrawal was codenamed Operation *Aster*. It began with evacuating elements of the German formations and Estonian civilians. In less than a week some 50,000 troops and 1,000 POWs had been removed. The remaining parts of Army Group North were ordered to withdraw into Latvia through the town of Parnu. The German III Armored Corps reached the town on September 20, exhausted and low on ammunition. The Soviets, with overwhelming superiority, advanced across the plains of Estonia, using both fields and the long, straight highway to soon reach Tallinn. Facing the advancing Soviets was the German II Army Corps that was comprised of ad hoc panzergrenadiers, Luftwaffe field units, Waffen-SS and Estonian conscripts, all trying in vain to slow the enemy onslaught.

Soldiers of the Nordland Division take cover at the side of the road. Soviet *jabos*—dive-bombers—were a constant threat.

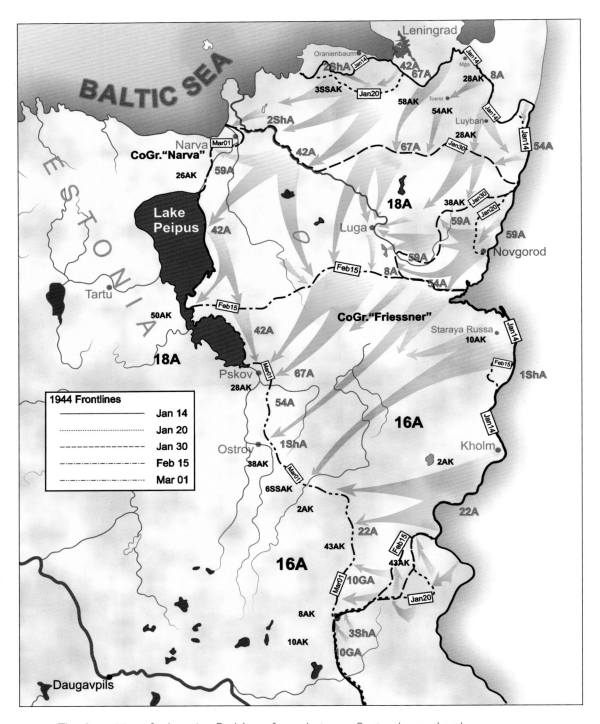

The disposition of advancing Red Army forces between September and early November 1944. By the end of October, it clearly shows that the Red Army had reached Tallinn, Riga, and the seaport of Memel, trapping the Sixteenth (16A) and Eighteenth (18A) Armies in what became known as the Courland pocket. It shows counterattacks from the pocket area in Tukums.

RED ARMY ORDER OF BATTLE SEPTEMBER 1944

1st Baltic Front (General Ivan Baghramin)

5th Guards Tank Army (General Vasily Volsky)

6th Guards Army (Lieutenant-General Ivan Chistyakov)

4th Shock Army (Lieutenant-General Pyotr Malyshev)

43rd Army (Lieutenant-General Afanasy Beloborodov)

51st Army (Lieutenant-General Yakov Kreizer)

33rd Army (Lieutenant-General Vyacheslav Tsvetayev)

3rd Air Army

2nd Baltic Front (Army General Andrey Yeryomenko)

3rd Shock Army (Lieutenant-General Nikolai Simoniak)

22nd Army (Lieutenant-General Vladimir Vostrukhov)

3rd Baltic Front (Colonel-General I.I. Maslennikov)

3rd Belorussian Front (parts) (Army General Ivan Chernyakhovsky)

2nd Shock Army (Lieutenant-General Porfiry Chanchibadze, then Lieutenant-General Ivan Fedyuninsky)

3rd Guards Mechanized Corps (Lieutenant-General Viktor Obukhov)

61st Army (Lieutenant-General Pavel Belov)

67th Army (Lieutenant-General Vladimir Sviridov)

Leningrad Front (parts) (Marshal L.A. Govorov)

8th Army (Lieutenant-General Filipp Starikov)

GERMAN ARMY ORDER OF BATTLE SEPTEMBER 1944

Army Group North (Colonel-General Ferdinand Schörner)

Army Detachment Narva (General Grasser)

Eighteenth Army (General Loch)

Sixteenth Army (General Hansen)

502nd Heavy Panzer Battalion

Army Group Center (Colonel-General Reinhardt)

Third Panzer Army (Colonel-General Erhard Raus)

XXXIX Panzer Corps

XXXX Panzer Corps

Panzergrenadier Division Grossdeutschland

4th Panzer Division

5th Panzer Division

17th Panzer Division

On September 22, Tallinn was abandoned. Some of the Estonian formations then changed sides and began to attack the retreating Germans. As the Germans withdrew for their lives, heavy Soviet artillery batteries bombed the harbour at Haapsalu and Vormsi Island in order to prevent desperate German units from escaping by sea. The Soviet 8th Army, Leningrad Front, then went on to capture the remaining islands off the Estonian coast in a large amphibious attack, which was part of the *Moonsund* landing operation.

The next stage of the offensive began on October 5, 1944. The 1st Baltic Front was to drive remaining German formations westward through Shaulyay and into a small bridgehead at Memel. Within 48 hours of the attack commencing, Red Army units of the 5th Guards Tank Army and 43rd Army smashed headlong into the Third Panzer Army. It all happened so fast that the German command post was almost overrun. In a radical attempt to stabilize the situation and prevent the complete collapse of the front, Schörner ordered his divisions to construct defenses in the northern tip of Courland, where the Leningrad Front had less than 20 miles of water to cross after it had captured the Soerve Peninsula. Riga was now under heavy air and ground bombardment, but still Hitler protested and delayed giving up the Latvian capital.

From Riga to Liepāja Hitler refused to countenance a general withdrawal. More than 200,000 soldiers, the bulk members of the Sixteenth and Eighteenth Armies, slowly became

A Hummel crew pose during operations in Latvia in the summer of 1944.

Civilians are pressed to clear the streets of Riga of debris following repeated heavy aerial bombardments of the city by the Soviet air force.

In Profile:

Tank Commander Grossdeutschland, East Prussia, and Raupenschlepper Ost (Caterpillar Tractor East) Towing 7.5cm PaK Gun

A Pz.Kpfw. IV tank commander of the Grossdeutschland Panzergrenadier Division standing in his turret. In early August, the division was transferred to East Prussia from the Ukraine where it saw heavy fighting in the Baltic states. It suffered such high casualties in both men and armor that it was nearly destroyed during the battles in the Memel bridgehead. (Johnny Shumate)

A Raupenschlepper Ost (Caterpillar Tractor East) or RSO hauling a 7.5cm PaK gun during operations in Latvia. The vehicle, along with the antitank weapon, is painted in dark sand with a camouflage scheme of brown patches sprayed over the whole vehicle and gun. Foliage has been applied over parts of the RSO and ordnance for additional camouflage protection. (Oliver Missing)

entrenched and cut off from East Prussia. In order to build sufficient defensible positions, Schörner ordered the withdrawal of his troops from Riga, and on October 13, the city fell to the 3rd Baltic Front. With the fall of the Latvian capital came the evacuation of thousands of troops and 100,000 tons of equipment into what became known as the Courland bridgehead. In total some 33 divisions of Army Group North were forced to retreat to the more defensible Courland position, and fight to the death for what remained of Latvian territory.

Over the next few weeks, the German Latvian front stabilized as the Red Army prepared to launch an offensive to crush the German forces in Courland and break through the German front toward Skrunda and Saldus. The attack was to coincide with the massive offensive being prepared in the central sector of the Eastern Front against German formations holding the banks of the Vistula in Poland.

When the Red Army finally launched their attack on October 27, Soviet forces also attacked southeast of Liepāja in an attempt to capture the port. Some 80 divisions assaulted strong German positions across a 10-mile front, but the defenses managed to hold and the Red Army stalled after only a few miles.

The German front once again was temporarily restored, allowing units to be resupplied, and to also evacuate the large numbers of wounded soldiers and civilians back to Germany. Yet, Schörner knew that success was futile and along certain sectors of the front, he began

Red Army soldiers march through Riga following its capture on October 24, 1944.

Soviet troops, carrying bouquets of flowers, parade through Riga.

ordering thousands of able-bodied troops and large numbers of antitank and heavy artillery guns to be transported back to the homeland. This significantly reduced German strength along the front and inside "Fortress Courland."

Slowly and inexorably Soviet troops were pressing Army Group North into Latvia, mainly compressed into the Courland pocket. Those German divisions that had not withdrawn from Estonia were either surrounded or annihilated in the face of unprecedented armor and massed infantry. By the autumn Soviet forces had reconquered Estonia following fierce battles in the northeast of the country on the Narva River and what was left of the Tannenberg Line.

2nd Baltic Front SU-152 tanks ford a river in Latvia.

Whilst the Germans continued resisting in Latvia, much of Lithuania had fallen into Soviet hands and what remained were isolated pockets of German resistance. In the Lithuanian town of Memel German divisions had fortified the seaport. The port had been initially utilized for resupply, but now the Germans were using if for both reinforcements and evacuation.

The defense of Memel was undertaken by the German XXVIII Corps under the command of General Hans Gollnick. The corps was part of the northern wing of the Third Panzer Army which was facing the 1st Baltic Front. The 58th Infantry Division would hold the northern part of the bridgehead perimeter, the 7th Panzer Division would hold the center, and the Grossdeutschland was to secure the southern part.

Yet, in spite of the dogged resilience of the troops defending Memel, Red Army attacks were relentless. The Soviet 43rd Army drove at speed past the southern edge of Memel and pushed its units on to the coast, which cut off Memel from the rest of the Baltics.

Horst Messer, a wounded German panzer soldier at Memel, wrote:

> On October 6, 1944 the Russians attacked, broke through south of our front and penetrated as far as Memel. Our Army Group was cut off and encircled by this move. On 28 October there began the first of the six so-called battles of Courland— bloody butchery which by the end of November 1944 had cost 70,000 German soldiers and the same number of Russians their lives ... We "seriously wounded" were loaded aboard a bus standing ready to convey us to the port of Libau. Here a hospital ship waited. Had I left as ordered, probably in a couple of days I would have been returned to the front. Instead, that evening I was in a convoy crossing the Baltic on course for home. The whole ship was full of wounded. Because I was actually only lightly wounded, I hung around the upper deck in case of torpedo attack. This was because I had no desire to go down in this steel coffin; I would have preferred to jump in the ice-cold water, for which purpose everybody had been given a lifejacket. When a submarine alarm was actually given, the mood of patients and crew fell to rock bottom. The fear can hardly be imagined—in the middle of the Baltic in icy temperatures, expecting the ship to be sunk by a torpedo at any moment. We were lucky, however, for nothing happened.

While many troops were withdrawn from Memel or had escaped encirclement, Hitler ordered that Memel be held at all costs. On October 14, Soviet forces launched a number of heavy attacks in order to try and seize the port, but failed. Luckily for the defenders the Red Army then shifted their offensive operations around Courland and their advance on East Prussia. The defense of Memel continued.

Horst Messer was indeed fortunate. On January 30, 1945, Captain Alexander Marinesko and Soviet submarine *S-13* were tracking the MV *Wilhelm Gustloff*, which had just evacuated some 10,500 people from Danzig. Of the total number of people on board, 173 were crew, around 9,000 were civilians, and the balance military personnel. At around 2100 hours, Marinesko had the ship in his sights and fired four torpedoes; one failed to detonate but the other three slammed into the *Wilhelm Gustloff*'s port side. Within 40 minutes the ship had sunk, with only about 1,000 people rescued. A few days later *S-13* claimed another victim, the *General von Steuben*, which took some 4,500 people to the bottom with her. To this day the *Wilhelm Gustloff* remains the largest ever maritime disaster in history.

German troops pass by a knocked-out Soviet IS-2 tank during bloody street fighting in Jelgava, Latvia. In late July, the Red Army launched an assault toward Jelgava and Tukums in order to cut off and encircle Army Group North. Jelgava was declared a fortress (*Festung*) and despite most of the garrison fleeing, fanatical defenders managed to hold out until October 10.

Panzergrenadiers are seen passing a stationary Panther during winter operations in Army Group North in 1944. (Michael Cremin)

The Winter Battles

The third phase of the fighting in the Courland bridgehead was known by the Latvian forces defending the area as the "Christmas battles." The first attack was unleashed by the Red Army on December 21, with a sustained assault near the town of Saldus. The Soviet 1st and 2nd Baltic Fronts commenced the attack by driving fast-moving armor and infantry toward the Courland perimeter in an attempt to blockade it. Defending the positions in front of the perimeter was the 19th SS Latvian Division. The Soviets had at least a six-to-one numerical superiority against their Latvian enemy but were content to bombard the front, probing for weak areas to break through. For hours Soviet aircraft bombed the German and Latvian lines and almost succeeded in cutting the lines near Ventspils. However, following a series of German counterattacks, the Red Army once again stalled with heavy losses, and the front, for the interim, was stabilized on New Year's Eve.

With the Germans now attempting to regroup following the initial offensive, every soldier was fully aware of the significance if the front collapsed. Not only would the coastal garrisons be cut off and eventually destroyed, but also masses of civilian refugees would be prevented from escaping by sea. Hitler made it quite clear that all remaining Wehrmacht,

A Soviet military map showing the Courland pocket and the Red Army surrounding it between October 1944 and May 1945.

A typical defensive position in Courland with an 8.8cm flak gun being used against an enemy ground position.

Waffen-SS volunteer units, and Luftwaffe personnel were not to evacuate, but to stand and fight and wage an unprecedented battle of attrition. He was determined to prevent the Red Army from spilling out of the Baltic states, capturing East and West Prussia, taking the ancient Teutonic city of Danzig and driving its mighty forces into the heartland of Pomerania. What Hitler was trying to avoid was a desperate defense along the frontier of the Reich by planning on drawing as much as possible of the main Soviet thrust away from its concerted effort on Berlin. It was for this reason the Führer made it known to his commanders in the field that their troops would have to defend their meager positions with every drop of blood if they were to avert a complete disaster in the Baltics.

In early January 1945, German formations restrengthened their defensive positions as the Soviet Army prepared for another winter offensive. On January 12/13, the Germans

The crew of an 8.8cm gun dismantle their weapon which will be hauled by the nearby halftrack.

RED ARMY ORDER OF BATTLE FEBRUARY 1945

1st Baltic Front (Army General Ivan Bagramyan)

51st Army (Army General Yakov Kreizer)

6th Guards Army (Colonel General Ivan Chistyakov)

4th Shock Army (Army General Pyotr Malyshev)

42nd Army (Lieutenant General Vladimir Petrovich Sviridov)

1st Shock Army (Lieutenant General Vladimir N. Razuvaev)

10th Guards Army (Lieutenant General Mikhail Kazakov

were engulfed in a storm of fire. Across the snow-covered terrain Soviet troops and massed armor poured onto the battlefield. From the north, on 3rd Belorussian right flank, the 1st Baltic Front attacked the Third Panzer Army on the Neman, as well as destroying its small bridgehead at Memel. The 3rd Belorussian's left flank was supported by the 2nd Belorussian Front, which had been ordered to drive northwest to the River Vistula, through the lines of the German Second Army, with the main objective of sealing off the whole of East Prussia.

German commanders in the field now resigned themselves to the gloomy prospect of losing the Baltic states; the news sent shock waves through the German high command. For them it marked the beginning of the Soviet invasion of the Fatherland. As German forces fought to delay the inevitable capture of the Baltics, the main bulk of the Red Army drive bypassed the various pockets of resistance and spilled out into the eastern provinces of Estonia and Latvia, where it fought a number of hard-pressed battles.

A light MG 42 machine gun crew during a fire mission against an enemy target. Note that gunner number two is feeding the ammunition belt. (Michael Cremin)

In Profile:

Panther Ausf.A and Waffen-SS Sturmmann

Panther Ausf.A defending the Courland perimeter in January 1945. The tank is painted in whitewash but its color is worn and the sand base camouflage scheme is coming through. (Oliver Missing)

A Waffen-SS Sturmmann during a defensive action in early 1945, near Memel. He is armed with the Karbiner 98K bolt action rifle. He wears the Waffen-SS standard camouflage *Erbsentarn* or dot 44 peas pattern reversible winter jacket. (Johnny Shumate)

A unit of winter-clad grenadiers belonging to Army Group Courland have halted on a snowy road and tuck into some rations before resuming their march. (Michael Cremin)

Positions around Courland were heavily attacked. For troops defending the pocket it was inevitable that every soldier had to continue to stand and fight to the bitter end. The significance of the defense of Courland was so paramount that on January 15, 1945, Hitler renamed Army Group North Army Group Courland, commanded by Colonel-General Lothar Rendulic. Just prior to the Red Army offensive, Hitler had redeployed several divisions back to Germany; he'd also included Schörner, who had been summoned home to help in the defense of the Reich. He was replaced by Rendulic.

In spite of Rendulic taking command, the situation was already on the point of disintegration. The army group was trapped inside Latvia and Soviet forces were continuing to try and reduce the Courland pocket by hammering against against the Baltic coast in the west, the Ibre Strait in the north, and the Gulf of Riga in the east. The strain on

A Soviet soldier drinks either soup, warm water, or vodka. The Red Army were masters in winter warfare and utilized the weather and terrain as an ally.

An ISU-152 with striped white camouflage markings painted over its armor during the early stages of the winter offensive in January 1945.

the troops trapped in the pocket managed to see Rendulic get permission from Hitler to withdraw seven divisions from Courland. The 4th Panzer Division, 31st, 32nd, 93rd Infantry Divisions, 11th SS Division Nordland, and the remnants of the worn-out 227th, 218th, and 389th Infantry Divisions including the 15th Latvian SS Division were evacuated by sea.

Those troops left out on the battlefield had resigned themselves to fight to the death, unconvinced by their commander's optimism that they were capable of stemming the enemy onslaught. Instead, they fought day to day, poorly armed and undermanned. They were clearly aware of the significance of losing their position in Latvia.

An MG 42 machine gun crew take cover in a bomb crater. They are looking skyward at probable enemy aircraft that constantly attacked the German front lines. By 1945 many units had become totally dependent on the MG 42 to hold back the enemy. (Michael Cremin)

GERMAN ARMY GROUP NORTH ORDER OF BATTLE, FEBRUARY 1945

Army Group North (to January 25, 1945)

Army Group Courland (January 25, 1945 to May 8, 1945)

(Colonel-General Heinrich von Vietinghoff; Colonel-General Lothar Rendulic from March 10, 1945; Colonel-General Carl Hilpert from March 25, 1945)

Sixteenth Army

(Colonel-General Carl Hilpert from March 10, 1945; General Ernst-Anton von Krosigk (KIA); General Friedrich-Jobst Volckamer von Kirchensittenbach from March 16)

<u>XVI Army Corps</u> (Lieutenant-General Ernst-Anton von Krosigk; Lieutenant-General Gottfried Weber from March 10)

81st Infantry Division (Lieutenant-General Franz Eccard von Bentivegni)

300th Infantry Division z.b.V. (Major-General Anton Eberth)

21st Luftwaffe Field Division (Lieutenant-General Albert Henze; Major-General Otto Barth from February 16, 1945)

<u>VI SS Army Corps</u> (SS-Obergruppenführer Walter Krüger)

24th Infantry Division (Major-General Harald Schultz)

12th Panzer Division (Lieutenant-General Erpo von Bodenhausen; Major-General Horst von Usedom from April 14, 1945)

19th SS Grenadier Division (Lieutenant-General Bruno Streckenbach)

<u>XXXVIII Army Corps</u> (General Kurt Herzog)

122nd Infantry Division (Genera Friedrich Fangohr; Major-General Bruno Schatz from January 20, 1945

290th Infantry Division (Major-General Hans-Joachim Baurmeister; Major-General Carl Henke from April 25, 1945; Lieutenant-General Bruno Ortler from April 27, 1945)

329th Infantry Division (Lieutenant-General Konrad Menkel; Major-General Werner Schulze from January 1, 1945)

Eighteenth Army

(General Ehrenfried Boege)

<u>I Army Corps</u> (General Friedrich Fangohr; Lieutenant-General Christian Usinger from April 21, 1945)

218th Infantry Division (Lieutenant-General Viktor Lang; Major-General Ingo von Collani from December 25, 1944; Lieutenant-General Werner Ranck from May 1, 1945)

132nd Infantry Division (Lieutenant-General Herbert Wagner; Major-General Rudolf Demme from January 8, 1945)

<u>II Army Corps</u> (General Johannes Mayer, Lieutenant-General Alfred Gause from April 1, 1945)

263rd Infantry Division (Lieutenant-General)

563rd Volksgrenadier Division (Major-General Ferdinand Brühl; Major-General Werner Neumann from February 25, 1945)

<u>X Army Corps</u> (General Siegfried Thomaschki)

87th Infantry Division (Major-General Helmuth Walter, Lieutenant-General Mauritz Freiherr von Strachwitz from January 16, 1945)

126th Infantry Division (Lieutenant-General Gotthard Fischer; Major-General Kurt Hähling from January 5, 1945)

30th Infantry Division (Major-General Otto Barth; Lieutenant-General Albert Henze from January 30, 1945)

<u>L Army Corps</u> (General Friedrich Jobst Volckamer von Kirchensittenbach; Lieutenant-General Erpo von Bodenhausen from April 11, 1945)

205th Infantry Division (Major-General Ernst Biehler; Major-General Karl-Hans Giese from November 15, 1944)

225th Infantry Division (Lieutenant-General Walter Risse)

11th Infantry Division (Lieutenant-General Hellmuth Reymann; Lieutenant-General Gerhard Feyerabend from November 18, 1944)

14th Panzer-Division (Major-General Oskar Munzel; Major-General Martin Unrein from November 25, 1944, Colonel Friedrich-Wilhelm Jürgen from February 19, 1945, Colonel Paul Lüneburg from March 22, 1945; Colonel Karl-Max Grässel from March 25, 1945)

<u>Security Divisions</u>

52nd Security Division *Festung Libau* (Lieutenant-General Albrecht Baron Digeon von Monteton)

201st Security Division (Major-General Anton Eberth)

207th Security Division (only Staff)

Luftwaffe

Jagdgeschwader 54 (Colonel Dietrich Hrabak)

| Defeat

During the first weeks of January 1945, the German forces in Army Group Courland continued to rigidly commit everything it still had. However, despite the dogged resistance, there was no coherent strategy, and any local counteroffensives were often blunted with severe losses. The Soviets possessed too many tanks, antitank guns and aircraft, and the Germans remained incapable of causing any serious losses or delays.

A mortar soldier armed with the GrW 42 mortar. This weapon was an attempt to give German infantry units a close support weapon with greater performance and impact than the standard mortars issued to the infantry units. (Michael Cremin)

Little in the way of reinforcements reached the beleaguered Germans, and those left holding a defensive position had already been forced into various ad hoc panzer units that were simply thrown together with a handful of

Whitewashed Panther tank during the defense of East Prussia. Along the German front, in spite of fortified positions, which were manned with Pak guns and machine-gun emplacements, the Red Army advanced in their thousands regardless of the cost in life to their own ranks.

A winter-clad mortar crew poise before resuming their advance across snowy terrain. To Hitler the defense of the Baltic States was the last bastion of defense in the East before the Reich was invaded. Every soldier, he said, was to continue and "stand and fight" in an unprecedented battle of attrition. (Michael Cremin)

tanks and panzergrenadiers. Most of these hastily formed formations were short-lived: they were either completely annihilated or had received such a mauling that they were reorganized into a different ad hoc formation under a new commander.

Communication lines between Army Group North and Army Group Center were now completely severed. The Soviets with their overwhelming superiority continued to gradually push the Germans back against the Latvian coast while stubborn German resistance in the seaport of Memel continued.

A column of StuGs halted in the snow. Despite the StuG's proven tank-killing potential and its service on the battlefield, the vehicle gradually deprived both Wehrmacht and Waffen-SS infantry of the vital fire support for which the assault gun was originally built, in order to supplement the massive losses in the Panzerwaffe. By January 1945 conditions in the ranks of the Panzerwaffe were so bad that many vehicles were simply abandoned due to the lack of fuel or ammunition.

By mid-January constant infantry attacks supported by both heavy aerial and ground bombardments necessitated the Grossdeutschland and 7th Panzer Divisions be withdrawn after suffering heavy losses. They were replaced by the 95th Infantry Division, in the hope that it would temporarily hold back the Soviet forces.

Over the coming days the Soviets increased the intensity of their attacks which eventually compelled the battered divisions defending Memel to begin evacuation before it was completely encircled and annihilated. The remaining troops were withdrawn and evacuated to the Coroian Spit on January 27, 1945; the port fell to the Soviets a few hours later, leaving remnants of the three German divisions defending the town to be evacuated and redeployed to Samland to reinforce the defense there.

Farther west Soviet spearheads continued their drive, probing northeast to a few small pockets of land surrounding three ports: Libau in Courland, Pillau in East Prussia, and Danzig at the mouth of the Vistula. The German units defending these ports were understrength, their defensive capabilities depending desperately, and improbably, on the old Prussian and Silesian fortresses of Breslau, Stettin, Kustrin, Folburg, Insterburg, and Königsberg.

As panic and confusion swept the lines, Hitler reiterated to his commanders the importance of holding these fortresses and drew particular significance to the port of Libau in Courland. The port was vital, he said, for the resupply to those German forces still fighting in the Baltics.

The Red Army too were well aware of the importance of Courland and, on February 12, they began their fifth major attack on the port of Libau. Fighting raged in Dzukste and south of Liepāja where the Russians had massed 21 divisions. South of Tukums 11 divisions tried to break through the German front and take Courland, but still the fortress held in spite of a massed attack against the 19th Infantry Division.

Soviet tank men with their commander pore over a map.

In thick snow a German soldier wears his padded winter reversible white side out and is armed with the 98K bolt action rifle. (Michael Cremin)

Red Army losses in attempting to take Courland were huge: it is estimated that some 320,000 troops were killed, wounded, or captured, with little gain to show for their effort. Yet, in spite of these losses, the Soviets continued pressing home their attacks. For the Germans there seemed nothing available to them to hold back the Soviet might, except iron will and fortitude.

German resistance continued with fanatical determination; the troops remained formidable opponents, fighting for every bridge, castle, port, town, and village against the Red tide. But to the German soldier defending what remained of the Baltic states this was no normal retreat. They knew only too well that the Russians were determined to exact vengeance. As the Red Army steamrolled across Latvia and Lithuania into East Prussia and

A Waffen-SS 3.7cm Flak crew. These deadly guns were much respected by low-flying Russian airmen and were also particularly devastating against light vehicles, as well as troops caught in the open. The weapon also armed a variety of vehicles on self-propelled mounts where they could be moved from one sector of the defensive line to another quickly and efficiently.

across into Pomerania, it left a wake of rapine and devastation. In Germany the Propaganda Ministry made much of the horrors and brutalities of the Red Army. Now, as the Soviets ploughed through to the frontiers of the Reich, it proved all too true. The horrors of what the Nazis had inflicted on the Soviets would be fully replicated by those of the conqueror. For the Russians, it was time to settle old scores.

Slowly and systematically the German defensive positions along the coast were destroyed. Some positions still held, with soldiers trapped in the Courland pocket, but defenses were slowly disintegrating under Soviet pressure. In spite of appeals to evacuate the troops from the pocket, Hitler continued to forbid it. Instead, he promised, futilely of course, additional reinforcements.

Three photographs taken in sequence of the Waffen-SS Brigade Langemarck during a fire mission with their 8.8cm Flak gun. A typical SS panzer division during this period was armed with 12 heavy 8.8cm Flak pieces, while less-well-equipped SS grenadier divisions still only possessed one or two, or none at all.

During a lull in the fighting an SS soldier offers his comrade a cigarette. By the end of January 1945 German troops were exhausted from months of ceaseless combat. However, the situation had deteriorated far quicker than the German high command had anticipated.

Civilians departing Courland; this was part of Operation *Hannibal*, the German naval operation involving the evacuation by sea of German troops and civilians from Courland, East Prussia, and the Polish corridor from mid-January to May 1945.

In Profile

T-34/85 Tank and Magirus 3-ton Truck

A T-34-85 tank belonging to the 19th Tank Corps, 2nd Baltic Front, Courland, March 1945. This vehicle has received an application of whitewash paint that has been liberally applied by the crew over its dark green summer camouflage paint. (Oliver Missing)

Magirus 3-ton Wehrmacht truck driving through thick snow and ice carries vital supplies to the Courland pocket. (Oliver Missing)

A T-34 tank in a captured East Prussian town, part of the East Prussian offensive launched by the Soviet 2nd Belorussian Front. This sealed the fate of German forces in the Baltics.

Elsewhere along the Baltics the Soviets continued pressing west in what they called their East Prussian Offensive. They had cut off Army Group Courland which allowed them (the Soviets) to advance swiftly through Lithuania and into East Prussia with devastating effect. By March they had captured Danzig, Zoppot, and Gotenhafen. As the front collapsed Hitler reluctantly conceded that the situation in the Baltic region was now so perilous that an invasion of the Reich was imminent.

In order to strengthen their defenses the remaining coastal ports were heavily fortified so that they could evacuate, resupply troops, and try to contain the Red Army's remorseless

Walking wounded Soviet infantry march through a captured town.

Waffen-SS Nordland troops prior to their evacuation by sea. From late October to December 1944, the Nordland remained in the Courland pocket. Divisional strength had been reduced to 9,000 men. In January 1945, the division was ordered to the Baltic port of Libau where it was evacuated by sea. Its remnants were sent to Berlin in April 1945.

drive. At Swinemünde the port there was heavily defended by Fortress Division Swinemünde. It was a very important naval base and home to the German rocket facility. On March 12, the seaport, naval base, and rocket facility were heavily bombed, killing some 23,000 people, including many refugees.

Waffen-SS MG 34 machine-gun crew on the front.

Soviet T-34-85 tanks and crews rest up in a forest before resuming the offensive. Foliage has been attached to the vehicle in the foreground in order to break up its distinctive shape.

The Fortress Division formed the northern anchor of the Third Panzer Army, and was used to protect the northern shores of the Baltic against the advancing Red Army. For weeks the fortress held out whilst the Soviets occupied large areas around the port.

By the end of March, the military situation for the Germans had deteriorated further. The position had become so bad that Hitler was forced to allow the Fourth Army to retreat across the Frisches Haff to the Nehrung.

A column of T-34 tanks halted along a muddy road. German units were overwhelmed by the never-ending stream of Soviet tanks and reserves.

A stationary Panther tank during the defense of Memel, which finally collapsed at the end of January 1945. Remnants of the three German divisions defending the town were evacuated and redeployed to Samland to reinforce the defense there.

In early April remnants of the German Second Army were renamed Army of East Prussia. Its forces were now hemmed in around the Bay of Danzig from Samland and Königsberg to the mouth of the Vistula. The remnants of two corps were given the task of holding positions north of Gotenhafen on the Hel Peninsula. Hitler demanded that it be held at all costs. He instructed all units in the Army of East Prussia and Army Group Courland to hold the front in order to draw the maximum enemy forces against the two armies and away from the main Soviet drive into Germany. But in spite of dogged resistance in many places, the Germans no longer had the manpower, war plant, or transportation to defend its positions effectively. The Red Army had effectively won the battle in the Baltics, and all that remained was mopping up isolated pockets of resistance.

The battle of Königsberg, also known as the Königsberg offensive, was one of the last operations of the East Prussian Offensive. The 1st Baltic and the 3rd Belorussian Fronts captured the city on April 9, 1945 following a two-month siege.

Soviet soldiers including an officer on horseback pick their way around a knocked-out StuG. III in the decimated city of Königsberg following its capture.

| Epilogue

The Baltic Offensive left hundreds of thousands of German soldiers and civilians cut off and besieged in East Prussia, on the Courland peninsula, and around Danzig. Many soldiers and civilians were wounded, sick, or starving, and all faced inevitable death or capture by the Soviets.

A column of sombre German POWs following the capture of Königsberg. By February 1945 German forces in the East had been driven back to the Oder River, the last line of defense before Berlin.

German POWs trudge past a stationary Soviet ISU-152 and T-34/85 tank, March 1945.

Already Operation *Hannibal*, the German naval evacuation of German troops and civilians, had witnessed the loss of some 158 merchant vessels during the 15-week course of the operation.

Yet, in spite of the losses, from May 1 to May 8, over 150,000 people were evacuated from the beaches of Hela alone. More than two million Germans are estimated to have been evacuated from the East during the operation, with around three-quarters of them being civilians and the balance military personnel. The operation is arguably the greatest sea evacuation in history and remarkably the troops managed to move out large quantities of equipment too. But despite the evacuation, the battle of the Baltics had been irretrievably lost. On May 8, remnants of Army Group Courland officially surrendered to Soviet forces. Two days later the Leningrad Front captured the Courland peninsula, reaching the coast off Riga Bay and the Baltic Sea. Some 140,500 troops including 28 generals in the Courland pocket capitulated.

The Baltic operations had cost thousands of lives. The Germans had fought for months against overwhelming odds. During this time, they had defended isolated areas for weeks and even months on end. The Courland defensive action was one of the longest military sieges of the war. The Narva front, too, saw many soldiers sacrificed, all trying fiercely to hold ground and stem the Red Army drive in reaching the Baltic Sea.

Although Hitler's "Halt" order had slowed down the Russian spearheads and tied down vast masses of men and equipment, the Soviet *Bagration* offensive in June 1944 against Army Group Center caused insurmountable problems for Army Group North. The offensive was so devastating it not only smashed German divisions in the center, it brought large Red Army formations thundering into Latvia and Lithuania, consequently rupturing defenses in Army Group North, and forcing troops to withdraw or become isolated. And so was the fate of the Fatherland sealed.

| Further Reading

Adair, Paul (1994, 2004). *Hitler's Greatest Defeat: The Collapse of Army Group Center, June 1944*. London: Weidenfeld Military.

Beevor, Antony & Luba Vinogradova (eds.) (2006). *A Writer at War: Vasily Grossman with the Red Army*. London: Pimlico.

Bruoygard, Terje (2013). "Operation Art in Theory and War: A Comparison of Soviet Theory and the Red Army's Conduct in Operation Bagration, 1944." Quantico, VA: USMC Command and Staff College. Retrieved 29 January 29, 2017.

Dunn, Walter S. (2000). *Soviet Blitzkrieg: The Battle for White Russia, 1944*. Boulder, CO: Lynne Rienner Publishers.

Glantz, David M. & Elizabeth Glantz (2016). *The Battle for Belorussia: The Red Army's Forgotten Campaign of October 1943–April 1944*. Kansas: University of Kansas Press.

Heeresgruppe Nord Diary 1944 [Baltics] 3211/Berlin Archives.

Jones, Richard M. (2021) *The 50 Greatest Shipwrecks*. Barnsley: Pen & Sword.

Krivosheev, G.F. (1997). *Soviet Casualties and Combat Losses in the Twentieth Century*. London: Greenhill Books.

Mazower, Mark (2008). *Hitler's Empire: Nazi Rule in Occupied Europe*. London: Allen Lane.

Merridale, C. (2006). *Ivan's War: Inside the Red Army, 1939–45*. London: Faber.

Mitcham, S. (2007) *German Defeat in the East 1944–45*, Mechanicsburg, PA. Stackpole.

Newton, Steven H. (1995). *Retreat from Leningrad: Army Group North, 1944/1945*. Philadelphia, PA: Schiffer Books.

Niepold, Gerd (1987). Translated by R. Simpkin. *Battle for White Russia: The Destruction of Army Group Center. June 1944*. London: Brassey's.

Tieke, Wilhelm (2001). *Tragedy of the Faithful: A History of the III. (Germanisches) SS-Panzer-Korps*. Winnipeg: J.J. Fedorowicz.

Zaloga, S. (1996). *Bagration 1944: The Destruction of Army Group Center*. Oxford: Osprey.

Zetterling, Niklas & Anders Franksson (1998). "Analyzing World War II Eastern Front Battles." *The Journal of Slavic Military Studies*. Abingdon, Oxfordshire: Routledge Taylor & Francis Group.

German officers being led away with their hands up past a stationary T-34 tank following their capture. The carnage of battle is still evident with smouldering military hardware sprawled along the road.

| Index